AQA Anthology of Poetry

Power and Conflict

AQA's *Power and Conflict* poetry cluster has its fair share of poems about war — and writing essays about them can be a real battle.

Not to worry. This brilliant book guides you through the entire cluster — form, structure, language, themes, context... the lot. And because it's from CGP, we get straight to the point, with no needless rambling.

We've also included plenty of practice questions to test you on what you've learned, plus a whole section of advice to help you write top-grade answers. Everything you need to power through the exams!

The Poetry Guide

Contents

How To Use This Book 1

Section One — The Poems

Ozymandias — Percy Bysshe Shelley 2
London — William Blake 4
The Prelude: Stealing the Boat — William Wordsworth 6
My Last Duchess — Robert Browning 8
The Charge of the Light Brigade — Alfred Tennyson 10
Exposure — Wilfred Owen 12
Storm on the Island — Seamus Heaney 14
Bayonet Charge — Ted Hughes 16
Remains — Simon Armitage 18
Poppies — Jane Weir 20
War Photographer — Carol Ann Duffy 22
Tissue — Imtiaz Dharker 24
The Emigrée — Carol Rumens 26
Kamikaze — Beatrice Garland 28
Checking Out Me History — John Agard 30
Practice Questions 32

Section Two — Themes

Power of Humans 36
Power of Nature 37
Effects of Conflict 38
Reality of Conflict 39
Loss and Absence 40
Memory 41
Negative Emotions 42
Identity 44
Individual Experiences 45
Practice Questions 46

Section Three — Poetic Techniques

Forms of Poetry 49
Poetic Devices 50
Use of Sound 52
Imagery 53
Rhyme and Rhythm 54
Voice 55
Beginnings of Poems 56
Endings of Poems 57
Mood 58
Practice Questions 59

Contents

Section Four — Exam Advice

The Poetry Exam 62
How to Structure Your Answer 63
How to Answer the Question 64
Planning Your Answer 67
Sample Answer 68

Section Five — Improving and Marking Sample Answers

Adding Quotes and Developing Points 70
Mark Scheme 72
Marking Answer Extracts 73
Marking a Whole Answer 75

Glossary 77
Index 79
Answers 80

Published by CGP

Editors:
Claire Boulter
Catherine Heygate
Matt Topping

With thanks to Jennifer Underwood and Nicola Woodfin for the proofreading.
With thanks to Laura Jakubowski for the copyright research.

Acknowledgements:

Cover quote from 'The Charge of the Light Brigade' by Alfred Tennyson

'Exposure' from *Wilfred Owen: The War Poems*, edited by Jon Stallworthy (Chatto and Windus, 1994)

'Storm on the Island' by Seamus Heaney from *Opened Ground.* Reprinted by permission of the publishers Faber and Faber Ltd.

'Bayonet Charge' by Ted Hughes from *Collected Poems.* Reprinted by permission of the publishers Faber and Faber Ltd.

'Remains' by Simon Armitage from *The Not Dead* (2008) reprinted by permission of Pomona Press.

'Poppies' by Jane Weir: Copyright Templar Poetry from *The Way I Dressed During the Revolution* (Templar, 2010)

'War Photographer' by Carol Ann Duffy from *Standing Female Nude* (1985), by permission of Anvil Press Poetry

'Tissue' by Imtiaz Dharker from *The Terrorist at my Table* published by Bloodaxe Books, 2006.
Reproduced with permission of Bloodaxe Books on behalf of the author.

'The Emigrée' by Carol Rumens from *Thinking of Skins* (1997) Bloodaxe Books, reprinted by permission of Carol Rumens.

'Kamikaze' by Beatrice Garland: Copyright Templar Poetry from *The Invention of Fireworks* (Templar, 2013)

'Checking Out Me History', John Agard. 'Checking Out Me History' copyright © 1996 by John Agard,
reproduced by kind permission of John Agard c/o Caroline Sheldon Literary Agency Ltd.

AQA material is reproduced by permission of AQA.

Every effort has been made to locate copyright holders and obtain permission to reproduce sources. For those sources where it has been difficult to trace the copyright holder of the work, we would be grateful for information. If any copyright holder would like us to make an amendment to the acknowledgements, please notify us and we will gladly update the book at the next reprint. Thank you.

ISBN: 978 1 78294 361 7
Printed by Elanders Ltd, Newcastle upon Tyne.
Clipart from Corel®

Based on the classic CGP style created by Richard Parsons.

How To Use This Book

This book is for anyone studying the 'Power and Conflict' cluster of the AQA GCSE English Literature Poetry Anthology. You'll have to answer an exam question on the poems — this book tells you what you need to know.

You need to know the poems really well

You need to know all fifteen poems in depth. Read each one carefully over and over again, and jot down your own ideas about it. This book will help you understand the poems and develop your ideas:

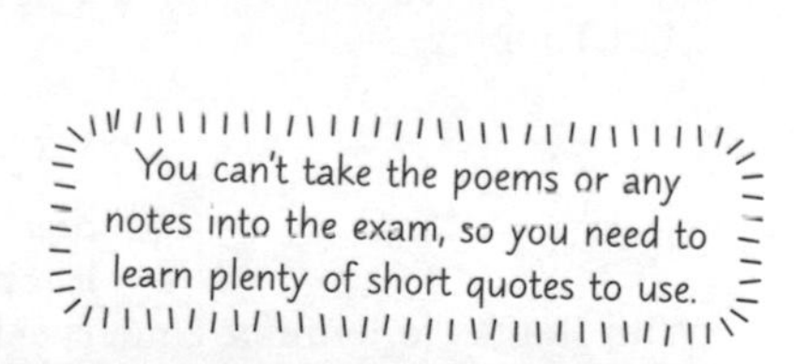

- Section One guides you through each poem in the cluster — read the notes on what each poem means, its main features, and the attitudes and feelings it conveys.
- Answer the questions about each poem — these will help you develop a personal response to it.
- When you feel that you know the poems well, have a go at the questions at the end of the section. They'll help you identify any gaps in your knowledge of the poems.

In the exam, you'll have to compare poems with a similar theme

1) The Poetry Anthology question will give you one poem from the 'Power and Conflict' cluster, and ask you to choose another with a similar theme to compare it to.
2) In Section Two the poems are grouped by theme, to give you some ideas of which poems you could compare in the exam and what you might say about them.
3) Have a go at the practice questions at the end of the section to check you're up to speed with the themes of each poem.

Have a look inside the front cover for a handy summary of which themes relate to which poems.

Get to grips with the main features of each poem

1) Section Three is all about form, structure and language.
2) It looks at how different poets use techniques like rhyme, rhythm and imagery to create effects — the examiners are really keen for you to write about this.
3) There are some more practice questions at the end of the section to help you test your knowledge.

First day on the job, and Tim had already got to grips with the 'self-destruct' feature of his car.

Learn how to write a cracking exam answer

1) You need to know how to write a great essay comparing two poems:
   - Section Four gives you loads of advice on how to plan and write a fantastic exam answer.
   - There are plenty of extracts from sample answers to show you the right way to approach the question.
2) Once you know the theory, put it into practice:
   - Section Five lets you test your skills by adding quotes or extending points to improve essay extracts. This will help you understand how to really use the poems to write a top-notch answer.
   - It also gives you some sample answers to grade, to help you work out how to improve your own answers.
3) There's no substitute for getting some practice at writing essays:
   - Use everything you've learnt to answer the exam-style questions at the end of Sections One, Two and Three.
   - You don't have to write a full essay for every question — making a detailed plan is still good practice.

Ozymandias

Shelley frames the poem as a story to make it clear that the narrator hasn't even seen the statue himself, he's only heard about it. This emphasises how unimportant Ozymandias is now.

Emphasises size and stature but also shows that the statue is incomplete.

The setting suggests an absence of life and vitality.

Ironic — even a powerful human can't control the damaging effects of time.

The sculptor understood the arrogance of the ruler.

I met a traveller from an antique land
Who said: 'Two vast and trunkless legs of stone
Stand in the desert. Near them, on the sand,
Half sunk, a shatter'd visage lies, whose frown,
5 And wrinkled lip, and sneer of cold command,
Tell that its sculptor well those passions read
Which yet survive, stamp'd on these lifeless things,
The hand that mock'd them and the heart that fed;
And on the pedestal these words appear:
10 "My name is Ozymandias, king of kings:
Look on my works, ye Mighty, and despair!"
Nothing beside remains. Round the decay
Of that colossal wreck, boundless and bare
The lone and level sands stretch far away.'

'Mock' can mean to ridicule, or to create a likeness of something — perhaps the sculptor intended his statue to make fun of Ozymandias.

Having "survive" and "lifeless" on the same line hints at how art can outlast human power, but the ruined statue shows that ultimately art can't immortalise power.

Arrogant and powerful — he even challenged other rulers.

Having a stressed syllable at the start of the line heightens Ozymandias's tone of command.

Irony — he tells other rulers to "despair" because of the size and grandeur of his "works", but in fact they should despair because their power is temporary and ultimately unimportant, like his.

The ruined statue shows how human achievements are insignificant compared to the passing of time.

Alliteration — emphasises the feeling of empty space in the surrounding desert.

The desert is vast and survives far longer than the broken statue, emphasising the insignificance of the statue and of Ozymandias.

Context — Shelley

Shelley was a 'Romantic' poet — 'Romanticism' was a movement that had a big influence on art and literature in the late 1700s and early 1800s. 'Romantic' poets believed in emotion rather than reason, tried to capture intense experiences in their work and particularly focused on the power of nature. Shelley also disliked monarchies, absolute power and the oppression of ordinary people. His radical political views were inspired by the events of the French Revolution, where the monarchy was overthrown.

POEM DICTIONARY

Ozymandias — another name for Ramesses II, a ruler of Ancient Egypt
antique — ancient
trunkless — without a torso
visage — face
pedestal — base of a statue
colossal — very large

Percy Bysshe Shelley

Percy Bysshe Shelley was a 'Romantic' poet, who only really became famous after his death. He wrote 'Ozymandias' in 1817, after hearing about how an Italian explorer had retrieved the statue from the desert.

You've got to know what the poem's about

1) The narrator meets a traveller who tells him about a statue standing in the middle of the desert.
2) It's a statue of a king who ruled over a past civilisation. His face is proud and he arrogantly boasts about how powerful he is in an inscription on the statue's base.
3) However, the statue has fallen down and crumbled away so that only the ruins remain.

Learn about the form, structure and language

1) **FORM** — The poem is a sonnet, with a turning-point (volta) at line 9 like a Petrarchan sonnet. However, it doesn't follow a regular sonnet rhyme scheme, perhaps reflecting the way that human power and structures can be destroyed. It uses iambic pentameter, but this is also often disrupted. The story is a second-hand account, which distances the reader even further from the dead king.
2) **STRUCTURE** — The narrator builds up an image of the statue by focusing on different parts of it in turn. The poem ends by describing the enormous desert, which helps to sum up the insignificance of the statue.
3) **IRONY** — There's nothing left to show for the ruler's arrogant boasting or his great civilisation. The ruined statue can be seen as a symbol for the temporary nature of political power or human achievement. Shelley's use of irony reflects his hatred of oppression and his belief that it is possible to overturn social and political order.
4) **LANGUAGE OF POWER** — The poem focuses on the power of Ozymandias, representing human power. However his power has been lost and is only visible due to the power of art. Ultimately, nature has ruined the statue, showing that nature and time have more power than anything else.
5) **ANGRY LANGUAGE** — The tyranny of the ruler is suggested through aggressive language.

Remember the feelings and attitudes in the poem

1) **PRIDE** — The ruler was proud of what he'd achieved. He called on other rulers to admire what he did.
2) **ARROGANCE** — The inscription shows that the ruler believed that he was the most powerful ruler in the land — nobody else could compete with him. He also thought he was better than those he ruled.
3) **POWER** — Human civilisations and achievements are insignificant compared to the passing of time. Art has the power to preserve elements of human existence, but it is also only temporary.

Go a step further and give a personal response

Have a go at answering these questions to help you come up with your own ideas about the poem:

Q1. Why do you think the poem is set in a vague "antique" land?
Q2. Why do you think "Nothing beside remains" comes directly after the ruler's proud inscription?
Q3. What does the poem suggest about the way Ozymandias ruled?
Q4. How might Shelley's status as a 'Romantic' poet have affected the tone of the poem?

Power of humans, power of nature, pride...

Compare Shelley's presentation of human power, pride, and life represented in art with Browning's in 'My Last Duchess'. The power of nature is also important in 'The Prelude', 'Exposure' and 'Storm on the Island'.

London

First-person narrator personalises the poem and makes it seem more real.

This sounds purposeless — could reflect how he feels powerless to change what's happening.

Means 'notice', but also suggests everyone he sees is marked by experience.

Suggests the whole city is affected, not just one area.

Even powerful, natural features like the River Thames are under human control, and affected by the city's problems.

Repetition emphasises feeling of bleakness — despair affects everyone and there's no relief from it.

I wander through each chartered street,
Near where the chartered Thames does flow,
And mark in every face I meet
Marks of weakness, marks of woe.

5 In every cry of every man,
In every infant's cry of fear,
In every voice, in every ban,
The mind-forged manacles I hear.

How the chimney-sweeper's cry
10 Every black'ning church appals,
And the hapless soldier's sigh
Runs in blood down palace walls.

But most through midnight streets I hear
How the youthful harlot's curse
15 Blasts the new-born infant's tear,
And blights with plagues the marriage hearse.

The speaker hears various distressing noises — makes this seem like a vivid, hellish experience.

People are trapped in every way, even by thoughts and attitudes.

Chimney sweeps were usually young boys — this is an emotive image of child labour.

Might be a reference to the French Revolution — sounds like he thinks ordinary people suffer while those in the palace are protected behind walls.

Seems to be angry at all forms of power — describing the church as "black'ning" could suggest that it is corrupt or that it is tarnished by its failure to look after people. It's also a grim visual image of the ugliness caused by the Industrial Revolution.

Contrast between innocence of youth and sordidness of prostitution.

He hears the prostitutes swearing, but he might also mean that they are a curse on London.

The innocence of newborn babies is lost immediately — society damages its members.

Powerful language of illness and disease. Destruction is implied by "blights", and "plagues" hints at something that's uncontrollable and destined to affect lots of people.

Oxymoron — links the happy image of marriage with death. Suggests that everything has been destroyed.

Context — 'Songs of Innocence and of Experience'
Blake wrote and illustrated two volumes of poetry which explored the state of the human soul. The 'Songs of Innocence' are positive poems which focus on childhood, nature and love, whereas the 'Songs of Experience' (including 'London') look at how that innocence is lost, and how society has been corrupted.

POEM DICTIONARY
chartered — mapped out or legally defined
woe — sadness
ban — can mean either 'a curse' or 'to prohibit'
manacles — handcuffs
hapless — unfortunate
harlot — a prostitute

William Blake

'London' was published in 1794. William Blake was an English poet and artist who held quite radical social and political views for the time — he believed in social and racial equality and questioned Church teachings.

You've got to know what the poem's about

1) The narrator is describing a walk round the city of London.
2) He says that everywhere he goes, the people he meets are affected by misery and despair.
3) This misery seems relentless. No one can escape it — not even the young and innocent.
4) People in power (like the Church, the monarchy and wealthy landowners) seem to be behind the problems, and do nothing to help the people in need.

Learn about the form, structure and language

1) **FORM** — This is a dramatic monologue — the first-person narrator speaks passionately and personally about the suffering he sees. The ABAB rhyme scheme is unbroken and seems to echo the relentless misery of the city. The regular rhythm could reflect the sound of his feet as he trudges around.
2) **STRUCTURE** — The narrator presents relentless images of downtrodden, deprived people. The first two stanzas focus on people he sees and hears, before the focus shifts in stanza three to the institutions he holds responsible. The final stanza returns to looking at people, showing how even newborn babies are affected.
3) **RHETORIC** — The narrator uses rhetorical language to persuade you of his point of view — he uses powerful, emotive words and images to reinforce the horror of the situation. Repetition is used to emphasise the number of people affected, and to show how society needs to change.
4) **USE OF THE SENSES** — The poem includes the depressing sights and sounds of the city — the first stanza is about what he sees, the second what he hears, and the last two stanzas combine the visual and aural.
5) **CONTRASTS** — These are used to show how everything is affected and nothing pure or innocent remains.

Remember the feelings and attitudes in the poem

1) **ANGER** — Emotive language and repetition show the narrator's anger at the situation. He mentions "every black'ning church" and "palace walls", suggesting he's especially angry at the people in power, who could do something to change things but don't.
2) **HOPELESSNESS** — The "mind-forged manacles" suggest that the people themselves are also to blame — they're trapped by their own attitudes. They appear hopeless because they're not able (or not even trying) to help themselves.

Go a step further and give a personal response

Have a go at answering these questions to help you come up with your own ideas about the poem:

Q1. Why do you think the poem is written in the first person?
Q2. What is the effect of repetition in the poem?
Q3. What does the phrase "mind-forged manacles" (line 8) suggest about the people of London?
Q4. What is the effect of setting the final stanza on "midnight streets"?

Individual experiences, anger, loss and absence...

'The Prelude' and 'The Emigrée' present contrasting individual experiences of a place — one is a negative experience of a rural environment and the other a positive experience of a remembered city.

The Prelude: Stealing the Boat

One summer evening (led by her) I found
A little boat tied to a willow tree
Within a rocky cave, its usual home.
Straight I unloosed her chain, and stepping in
5 Pushed from the shore. It was an act of stealth
And troubled pleasure, nor without the voice
Of mountain-echoes did my boat move on;
Leaving behind her still, on either side,
Small circles glittering idly in the moon,
10 Until they melted all into one track
Of sparkling light. But now, like one who rows,
Proud of his skill, to reach a chosen point
With an unswerving line, I fixed my view
Upon the summit of a craggy ridge,
15 The horizon's utmost boundary; far above
Was nothing but the stars and the grey sky.
She was an elfin pinnace; lustily
I dipped my oars into the silent lake,
And, as I rose upon the stroke, my boat
20 Went heaving through the water like a swan;
When, from behind that craggy steep till then
The horizon's bound, a huge peak, black and huge,
As if with voluntary power instinct,
Upreared its head. I struck and struck again,
25 And growing still in stature the grim shape
Towered up between me and the stars, and still,
For so it seemed, with purpose of its own
And measured motion like a living thing,
Strode after me. With trembling oars I turned,
30 And through the silent water stole my way
Back to the covert of the willow tree;
There in her mooring-place I left my bark, –
And through the meadows homeward went, in grave
And serious mood; but after I had seen
35 That spectacle, for many days, my brain
Worked with a dim and undetermined sense
Of unknown modes of being; o'er my thoughts
There hung a darkness, call it solitude
Or blank desertion. No familiar shapes
40 Remained, no pleasant images of trees,
Of sea or sky, no colours of green fields;
But huge and mighty forms, that do not live
Like living men, moved slowly through the mind
By day, and were a trouble to my dreams.

Unclear here who 'her' is. An earlier part of the poem suggests it's nature, personified.

Happy, rural image.

Narrator appears confident.

Seems familiar to him.

Oxymoron hints at the narrator's guilt.

The narrator knows he's doing something wrong — this is the first clue that something isn't quite right.

The succession of 'l' sounds helps the poem flow, like the boat moving gently across the lake.

Again, narrator seems confident, maybe a bit arrogant. This contrasts with the mood later in the poem.

This emptiness contrasts with line 22, when he looks at the horizon again. This makes the appearance of the mountain more shocking.

The metaphor of 'a fairy boat' makes the scene seem magical and otherworldly, but still not threatening.

The natural simile shows that he's confident and in control — enhances the contrast with the next line.

Turning-point (volta) introduces a complete change in tone. The simple word is emphasised by being at the start of the line and by the caesura.

A mountain appears on the horizon. Very different language now — darker and more threatening.

The mountain is personified. Ugly image — contrast to earlier beautiful images of the boat ('elfin', 'swan').

As the narrator rows away from the mountain, more and more of it comes into view. This means it seems like the mountain is getting bigger, and makes this sound like a nightmare.

The mountain is calm, powerful and in control — contrasts with the narrator's fear.

The repetition of sibilant sounds creates a sinister mood.

He's afraid and guilty, and wants to hide away — he feels like an intruder.

The event has had a big impact on him — 'grave' means serious, but may also be a reminder of his own mortality.

The impact was long lasting.

The vague language shows that the narrator doesn't understand what he's seen — he's struggling to describe it.

The narrator is left feeling alone and unsettled.

The narrator no longer thinks of nature in terms of pretty images — he's learnt there's more to it than that.

Nature is described as a powerful, conscious being that can influence our lives.

Unsettling image — helps us to empathise with him. Huge contrast to the tone and mood at start.

Context — 'The Prelude'

This is an extract from the first of fourteen books that make up Wordsworth's poem, 'The Prelude'. The book is entitled 'Introduction — Childhood and School-Time'. Wordsworth was a 'Romantic' poet (see p.2). Like other 'Romantic' poetry, this extract explores the connection between nature and human emotion, and the way human identity and character is shaped by experience.

POEM DICTIONARY

stealth — secrecy
pinnace — a small boat
lustily — enthusiastically
covert — shelter
bark — an old type of sailing boat

William Wordsworth

William Wordsworth was a poet from the Lake District. 'The Prelude' is an autobiographical poem — it explores key moments and experiences in Wordsworth's life. It was published shortly after his death in 1850.

You've got to know what the poem's about

1) The extract begins on a summer evening when the narrator finds a boat tied to a tree. He unties the boat and takes it out on the lake.
2) Initially the narrator seems happy and confident, and he describes a beautiful scene. A mountain appears on the horizon and the narrator is afraid of its size and power.
3) He turns the boat around and goes home, but his view of nature has changed.

The mountain scared Bill, but he wasn't sure why.

Learn about the form, structure and language

1) **FORM** — This extract is a first-person narrative. It sounds personal and describes a turning point in the poet's life. The use of blank verse (unrhymed verse in iambic pentameter) makes it sound serious and important, and the regular rhythm makes it sound like natural speech.
2) **STRUCTURE** — There are three main sections in the extract. In the first, the tone is fairly light and carefree. There's a distinct change when the mountain appears — the tone becomes darker and more fearful. In the final section, the narrator reflects on how the experience has changed him.
3) **BEAUTIFUL LANGUAGE** — The poem begins with a series of pretty, pastoral images of nature.
4) **CONFIDENT LANGUAGE** — The narrator appears sure of himself at first — almost arrogant in his view of himself and his place in the world. He gives the impression of feeling powerful.
5) **DRAMATIC LANGUAGE** — The initial glimpses of threatening language become more intense after the mountain appears. The narrator comes to understand how powerful nature is.
6) **FEARFUL LANGUAGE** — The narrator is far less confident at the end of the extract. He's troubled by the "huge and mighty forms" of nature he's glimpsed. The experience has a lasting, haunting effect on him.

Remember the feelings and attitudes in the poem

1) **CONFIDENCE** — The narrator feels comfortable and in control to start with, but his confidence in himself and the world around him is shaken by this one event.
2) **FEAR** — Nature is shown to be more powerful than a human being. The narrator is left with a feeling of awe and respect for nature, but he's also scared by it.
3) **REFLECTION** — The poem ends with the narrator reflecting on how he's been changed by the event. His thoughts and dreams are still troubled by what he's experienced.

Go a step further and give a personal response

Have a go at answering these questions to help you come up with your own ideas about the poem:

Q1. What does the phrase "troubled pleasure" (line 6) suggest about the narrator's actions and feelings?
Q2. What is the effect of the repetition of "and" in lines 24-29?
Q3. Can you empathise with the narrator? Is his reaction understandable?
Q4. What impression of nature do you have by the end of the poem?

The power of nature, fear, individual experiences...

Nature is presented as being very powerful and frightening in several other poems, including 'Exposure' and 'Storm on the Island'. The narrator of 'Remains' has also been changed by a personal experience.

My Last Duchess

Ferrara

That's my last Duchess painted on the wall,
Looking as if she were alive. I call
That piece a wonder, now: Frà Pandolf's hands
Worked busily a day, and there she stands.
5 Will't please you sit and look at her? I said
'Frà Pandolf' by design, for never read
Strangers like you that pictured countenance,
The depth and passion of its earnest glance,
But to myself they turned (since none puts by
10 The curtain I have drawn for you, but I)
And seemed as they would ask me, if they durst
How such a glance came there; so, not the first
Are you to turn and ask thus. Sir, 'twas not
Her husband's presence only, called that spot
15 Of joy into the Duchess' cheek: perhaps
Frà Pandolf chanced to say 'Her mantle laps
Over my lady's wrist too much,' or 'Paint
Must never hope to reproduce the faint
Half-flush that dies along her throat': such stuff
20 Was courtesy, she thought, and cause enough
For calling up that spot of joy. She had
A heart – how shall I say? – too soon made glad,
Too easily impressed; she liked whate'er
She looked on, and her looks went everywhere.
25 Sir, 'twas all one! My favour at her breast,
The dropping of the daylight in the West,
The bough of cherries some officious fool
Broke in the orchard for her, the white mule
She rode with round the terrace – all and each
30 Would draw from her alike the approving speech,
Or blush, at least. She thanked men, – good! but thanked
Somehow – I know not how – as if she ranked
My gift of a nine-hundred-years-old name
With anybody's gift. Who'd stoop to blame
35 This sort of trifling? Even had you skill
In speech – (which I have not) – to make your will
Quite clear to such an one, and say, 'Just this
Or that in you disgusts me; here you miss,
Or there exceed the mark' – and if she let
40 Herself be lessoned so, nor plainly set
Her wits to yours, forsooth, and made excuse,
– E'en then would be some stooping; and I choose
Never to stoop. Oh sir, she smiled, no doubt,
Whene'er I passed her; but who passed without
45 Much the same smile? This grew; I gave commands;
Then all smiles stopped together. There she stands
As if alive. Will't please you rise? We'll meet
The company below, then. I repeat,
The Count your master's known munificence
50 Is ample warrant that no just pretence
Of mine for dowry will be disallowed;
Though his fair daughter's self, as I avowed
At starting, is my object. Nay, we'll go
Together down, sir. Notice Neptune, though,
55 Taming a sea-horse, thought a rarity,
Which Claus of Innsbruck cast in bronze for me!

Context — Duke Alfonso II of Ferrara
Ferrara is a region of Italy. In 1561, the Duke of Ferrara's wife, Lucrezia, died in suspicious circumstances — there were rumours she was poisoned. Hearing about this event probably inspired Browning to write this poem.

Sounds as if he owns the Duchess herself, not just the picture of her.

Sets a sinister tone.

The name of the artist.

Sounds polite, but he's really being quite forceful here.

The punctuation doesn't end the line, with the Duke speaking again immediately — he doesn't give his visitor a chance to speak.

He controls who looks at the painting, but he couldn't control who looked at his wife when she was alive.

Suggests people were scared of his temper.

Creates the impression of a question from the visitor, but we hear it through the Duke — he's in complete control.

Reference to death is out of place and suspicious — it hints at the Duchess's fate.

Repeating this shows that his wife's blushes bother him.

The Duke struggles to express his irritation.

She flirted a lot — the Duke thinks so anyway.

She was cheery and friendly — but the Duke means this as a criticism.

Enjambment makes it sound as if he's getting carried away by his anger.

He sounds as if he's justifying himself — he's defensive.

The punctuation and repetition here creates a stuttering effect, which underlines his exasperation with her behaviour.

Repetition of "stoop" in lines 34, 42 and 43 hints at how the Duke felt his wife was beneath him.

He's proud of his history, his important family and the titles of "Duke" and "Duchess".

False modesty — he clearly does like speaking.

This word suggests he was more bothered about the Duchess's behaviour than he's letting on.

The Duke is so proud that even criticising his wife would have been beneath him — he believes she shouldn't need to be reminded how to behave.

He sounds suspicious of her — maybe he thought she was being unfaithful.

This seems to be a euphemism for his wife's murder. "I gave commands" is cold and cynical.

He's arranging his next marriage — his Next Duchess.

He returns to the subject of his art collection, which emphasises his power and wealth. The story of his last Duchess is a subtle warning to his visitor about how he expects his next wife to behave.

POEM DICTIONARY
countenance — face
durst — dare
mantle — cloak
bough — branch
officious — interfering
forsooth — indeed
munificence — generosity
dowry — money paid to a man by his bride's family when they marry
avowed — said
Neptune — Roman god of the sea

Robert Browning

Browning was born in England but lived in Italy for many years. He was fascinated by the Italian Renaissance (14th-16th centuries) — a period in which the arts flourished. 'My Last Duchess' was published in 1842.

You've got to know what the poem's about

1) The Duke proudly points out the portrait of the Duchess (his former wife) to a visitor.
2) The Duke was angered by the Duchess's behaviour — she was friendly towards everyone and he was annoyed that she treated him just like anyone else.
3) He acted to stop the Duchess's flirtatious behaviour, but he doesn't say how he did this. There are strong hints that he had her murdered.
4) The Duke and his guest walk away from the painting and the reader discovers that the Duke's visitor has come to arrange the Duke's next marriage.

Learn about the form, structure and language

1) **FORM** — The poem is a dramatic monologue written in iambic pentameter. This reinforces the impression that the Duke is in conversation with his visitor. The rhyming couplets show the Duke's desire for control, but the enjambment suggests that he gets carried away with his anger and passions. This creates a picture of a somewhat unstable character, whose obsession with power is unsettling.
2) **STRUCTURE** — The poem is framed by the visit to the Duke's gallery, but the Duke gets caught up in talking about the Duchess instead of just describing the art. The poem builds towards a kind of confession, before the identity of the visitor is revealed, and the Duke moves on to talking about another artwork.
3) **POWER AND OBJECTIFICATION** — The Duke felt the need to have power and control over the Duchess. He saw her as another of his possessions, to be collected and admired, just like his expensive artworks.
4) **DRAMATIC IRONY** — The things the Duke says about the Duchess seem quite innocent, but they often have more sinister meanings for the reader. There's a gap between what the Duke tells his listener, and what the poet allows us to read between the lines.
5) **STATUS** — Status is really important to the Duke. He cares about how others see him.

Remember the feelings and attitudes in the poem

1) **PRIDE** — The Duke is very proud of his possessions and his status.
2) **JEALOUSY** — He couldn't stand the way the Duchess treated him the same as everyone else (lines 31-34).
3) **POWER** — The Duke enjoys the control he has over the painting (lines 9-10). He didn't have this power over the Duchess when she was alive.

Go a step further and give a personal response

Have a go at answering these questions to help you come up with your own ideas about the poem:

Q1. Do you think the Duke ever had any affection for the Duchess? Why / Why not?
Q2. How is the Duke's view of himself different from the way the reader sees him?
Q3. Is the title of the poem effective? Why? Can you think of a suitable alternative title?
Q4. Why do you think the Duke is the only one who speaks in the poem?

Pride, power of humans...

Compare the Duke's pride and craving for power with the dead king's attitude and desires in 'Ozymandias'. You could also look at how the abuse of power is presented in this poem and 'Checking Out Me History'.

The Charge of the Light Brigade

I

Half a league, half a league,
Half a league onward,
All in the valley of Death
Rode the six hundred.
5 'Forward, the Light Brigade!
Charge for the guns!' he said:
Into the valley of Death
Rode the six hundred.

II

'Forward, the Light Brigade!'
10 Was there a man dismay'd?
Not tho' the soldier knew
Some one had blunder'd:
Theirs not to make reply,
Theirs not to reason why,
15 Theirs but to do and die:
Into the valley of Death
Rode the six hundred.

III

Cannon to right of them,
Cannon to left of them,
20 Cannon in front of them
Volley'd and thunder'd;
Storm'd at with shot and shell,
Boldly they rode and well,
Into the jaws of Death,
25 Into the mouth of Hell
Rode the six hundred.

IV

Flash'd all their sabres bare,
Flash'd as they turn'd in air
Sabring the gunners there,
30 Charging an army, while
All the world wonder'd:
Plunged in the battery-smoke
Right thro' the line they broke;
Cossack and Russian
35 Reel'd from the sabre stroke
Shatter'd and sunder'd.
Then they rode back, but not
Not the six hundred.

V

Cannon to right of them,
40 Cannon to left of them,
Cannon behind them
Volley'd and thunder'd;
Storm'd at with shot and shell,
While horse and hero fell,
45 They that had fought so well
Came thro' the jaws of Death
Back from the mouth of Hell,
All that was left of them,
Left of six hundred.

VI

50 When can their glory fade?
O the wild charge they made!
All the world wonder'd.
Honour the charge they made!
Honour the Light Brigade,
55 Noble six hundred!

The rhythm sounds like galloping horses' hooves — it gives the impression that the horses are unstoppable.

Sounds sinister — the reader is warned right from the start that something bad is going to happen.

The commanding officer is speaking here.

They're presented as one group with one purpose.

Soldiers realise the order was a mistake but do what they're told because it's their duty to obey orders. The poet respects them for this.

Rhyme and repetition emphasise the soldiers' obedience and sense of duty, even though they know they will almost certainly be killed.

There's a line in the Bible that says "Yea, though I walk through the valley of the shadow of death, I will fear no evil" (Psalm 23). Using Biblical references makes the poem seem solemn and significant.

Repetition at the start and end of the lines reflects the way the soldiers are surrounded by the enemy's guns. It also replicates the sound of gunfire.

Sibilance emphasises the idea of ammunition flying towards them.

These images personify death and hell and make them seem like monsters that the soldiers can't escape from.

The first three stanzas end with the same line. It adds to the sense of foreboding and reminds us of the number of soldiers.

The repetition of "Flash'd" and the rhyme create a powerful image of the cavalry using their swords.

This reminds us that the cavalry only had swords against the Russian guns.

Double meaning — could mean that people marvelled at their bravery or that they wondered why they had been sent on the charge. This poem was written in 1854 in response to a newspaper article about the battle. Many newspapers at the time were critical of the Crimean War, but this poem focuses on the bravery of the soldiers rather than the mistakes of the military leaders.

Several lines begin with verbs, emphasising the action and increasing the pace of the poem.

The sibilance here sounds vicious.

The repetition of "not" emphasises the fact that some of the brigade have been killed. It also creates a broken, stuttering effect, making it sound almost as if the speaker is upset.

Similar to the opening lines of stanza 3, but now the soldiers are retreating.

Powerful, onomatopoeic verbs suggest the noise from the cannons.

The sense of admiration is touched with sadness.

The repetition of "left of" reminds us that lives have been lost, and makes the poem sound sad.

This is a rhetorical question that challenges the reader.

Sounds dramatic and daring.

This command is repeated to leave the reader with the idea that they should honour the cavalry.

POEM DICTIONARY
sabres — long curved swords
sabring — to cut or wound with a sabre
battery — a group of cannons
Cossack — a warrior from southern Russia and Ukraine

Alfred Tennyson

Alfred Tennyson was one of the greatest poets of the Victorian era, and was Poet Laureate from 1850 until his death in 1892. He wrote this poem in 1854 as a tribute to the men who died in the battle it describes.

You've got to know what the poem's about

1) The poem describes a disastrous battle between British cavalry (soldiers on horseback) and Russian forces during the Crimean War (1853-1856).
2) A misunderstanding meant that the Light Brigade were ordered to advance into a valley surrounded by enemy soldiers.
3) The cavalry were only armed with swords, whereas the Russian soldiers had guns. The Light Brigade were virtually defenceless against their enemies, and many of them were killed.

Learn about the form, structure and language

1) **FORM** — The poem's narrated in the third person, making it seem like a story. The regular, relentless rhythm creates a fast pace, imitating the cavalry's advance and the energy of the battle. Rhyming couplets and triplets drive the poem forwards, but the momentum is broken by unrhymed lines, which could mirror the horses stumbling and soldiers falling. The overall lack of rhyme scheme hints at the chaos of war.
2) **STRUCTURE** — The poem tells the story of the battle in chronological order, from the charge of the men in the first three stanzas, to the battle in the fourth and the retreat in the fifth. The final stanza is shorter and summarises the heroism of the brigade.
3) **REPETITION** — Repetition creates a sense of impending doom and inevitability. Repetition of "six hundred" at the end of each stanza reinforces the idea of the large numbers of men involved, with the references to them summarising the story of the battle.
4) **HEROIC LANGUAGE** — Adverbs like "Boldly" and verbs like "Charging" emphasise the men's bravery. Respectful language shows how the narrator feels the soldiers should be remembered.
5) **VIOLENT LANGUAGE** — The narrator chooses powerful verbs and adjectives to give a strong sense of the violence of the battle, and uses sounds to create a vivid, noisy, hellish setting.

Remember the feelings and attitudes in the poem

Derek was relieved his horse hadn't learnt how to charge yet.

1) **ADMIRATION** — The narrator admires the bravery and sacrifice of the men because they obeyed orders even though they knew death was likely. He thinks that the world should recognise their bravery and appreciate their sacrifice.
2) **PATRIOTISM** — The men followed the orders because of their duty to their country, and the speaker portrays them as heroes for doing this.
3) **HORROR** — There's a suggestion that the narrator is horrified by the violence of the battle.

Go a step further and give a personal response

Have a go at answering these questions to help you come up with your own ideas about the poem:

Q1. How does the phrase "jaws of Death" (line 46) make you feel? Explain your answer.
Q2. How does the narrator convey the terror and violence of the battle?
Q3. Why do you think the stanzas in the poem are numbered?

Effects of conflict, reality of war...

'Poppies', 'Remains' and 'War Photographer' are all good poems to look at alongside this one if you're thinking about the effects of conflict. 'Bayonet Charge' and 'Exposure' work well for the reality of war.

Exposure

Our brains ache, in the merciless iced east winds that knive us...
Wearied we keep awake because the night is silent...
Low, drooping flares confuse our memory of the salient...
Worried by silence, sentries whisper, curious, nervous,
5 But nothing happens.

Watching, we hear the mad gusts tugging on the wire,
Like twitching agonies of men among its brambles.
Northward, incessantly, the flickering gunnery rumbles,
Far off, like a dull rumour of some other war.
10 What are we doing here?

The poignant misery of dawn begins to grow...
We only know war lasts, rain soaks, and clouds sag stormy.
Dawn massing in the east her melancholy army
Attacks once more in ranks on shivering ranks of grey,
15 But nothing happens.

Sudden successive flights of bullets streak the silence.
Less deathly than the air that shudders black with snow,
With sidelong flowing flakes that flock, pause, and renew;
We watch them wandering up and down the wind's nonchalance,
20 But nothing happens.

Pale flakes with fingering stealth come feeling for our faces –
We cringe in holes, back on forgotten dreams, and stare, snow-dazed,
Deep into grassier ditches. So we drowse, sun-dozed,
Littered with blossoms trickling where the blackbird fusses,
25 – Is it that we are dying?

Slowly our ghosts drag home: glimpsing the sunk fires, glozed
With crusted dark-red jewels; crickets jingle there;
For hours the innocent mice rejoice: the house is theirs;
Shutters and doors, all closed: on us the doors are closed, –
30 We turn back to our dying.

Since we believe not otherwise can kind fires burn;
Nor ever suns smile true on child, or field, or fruit.
For God's invincible spring our love is made afraid;
Therefore, not loath, we lie out here; therefore were born,
35 For love of God seems dying.

Tonight, this frost will fasten on this mud and us,
Shrivelling many hands, puckering foreheads crisp.
The burying-party, picks and shovels in shaking grasp,
Pause over half-known faces. All their eyes are ice,
40 But nothing happens.

This is a shared, painful experience.

Nature is personified and seems to be attacking them.

Lots of different emotions — another reason why their brains hurt.

Ellipses hint that they're waiting for something to happen — it never does.

The short, simple half line emphasises their boredom and tension.

The "brambles" of the barbed wire remind us of the pain caused by nature.

Assonance and onomatopoeia create a vivid aural description.

This is a Biblical reference to Matthew 24:6, where Jesus foretells the end of the world. He says "You will hear of wars and rumours of wars".

Rhetorical question asks what the point of it all is.

No colour — the battlefield is cold and lifeless. Grey was also the colour of German uniforms, so this aligns nature with the enemy.

Dawn is personified using the language of battle. Normally dawn brings hope, but not here.

The description of dawn approaching mirrors the soldiers in the trenches.

Sibilance mimics the whistling sound of bullets flying.

Snow is normally white (symbolising purity), but here it's black (symbolising evil or death).

Alliteration emphasises the relentlessness of the snow.

The snowflakes are personified — they're maliciously seeking the men's faces.

Another question, possibly answering the first question — they're here to die.

Half-rhyme creates a link between their current situation and their dreams of the past.

Assonance of long 'oh' sounds makes the imagined journey sound painful and slow.

The caesurae in this stanza create a division on each line, which reflects how the men are shut out of their homes. This also reflects the soldiers' concern that people back home were losing interest in their fate as the war dragged on.

Fires offer them no warmth — they look like jewels, which are precious but cold.

Suggests that they believe they're sacrificing themselves in order for life at home to be preserved.

Could mean that their love of God is disappearing, or that they feel God's love for them is dying.

Vivid image of what exposure to the cold does to their bodies.

Metaphor refers to the eyes of the living and the dead men — it's a vivid description of how they've been overpowered by nature. It hints that the living men are no longer able to feel any emotion.

Final stanza ends in same way as first stanza, suggesting that even death doesn't change anything.

POEM DICTIONARY
salient — a section of trenches that reached into enemy territory
sentries — soldiers watching for danger
glozed — a combination of 'glowing' and 'glazed'
poignant — painfully sad
loath — unwilling
puckering — contracting into wrinkles or folds

Wilfred Owen

Wilfred Owen wrote 'Exposure' in 1917-18 from the trenches of World War One, not long before he was killed in battle. Much of Owen's poetry reveals his anger at the war's waste of life and its horrific conditions.

You've got to know what the poem's about

1) Soldiers in the trenches of World War One are awake at night, afraid of an enemy attack.
2) However, nature seems to be their main enemy — it's freezing cold, windy and snowing.
3) The men imagine returning home, but the doors there are closed to them. They believe that sacrificing themselves in the war is the only way of keeping their loved ones at home safe.
4) They return to thinking about their deaths in the icy, bleak trenches.

Learn about the form, structure and language

1) **FORM** — The poem's written in the present tense using the first person plural (e.g. "Our", "We", "us"). This collective voice shows how the experience was shared by soldiers across the war. Each stanza has a regular rhyme scheme (ABBAC), reflecting the monotonous nature of the men's experience, but the rhymes are often half-rhymes (e.g. "snow" & "renew"). The rhyme scheme offers no comfort or satisfaction — the rhymes are jagged like the reality of the men's experience and reflect their confusion and fading energy. Each stanza ends with a half line, leaving a gap which mirrors the lack of activity or hope for the men.
2) **STRUCTURE** — The poem has eight stanzas, but there's no real progression — the last stanza ends with the same words as the first one, reflecting the monotony of life in the trenches and the absence of change.
3) **QUESTIONS** — The poem uses rhetorical questions to ask why the men are exposed to such dreadful conditions, and whether there's any point to their suffering.
4) **BLEAK LANGUAGE** — The poem includes lots of bleak imagery to remind the reader of the men's pain, the awful weather and the lack of hope for the soldiers. Assonance, onomatopoeia and carefully chosen verbs add to the bleak mood and make the descriptions vivid and distressing.
5) **PERSONIFICATION** — Nature is repeatedly personified, making it seem the real enemy in the war.

Remember the feelings and attitudes in the poem

1) **SUFFERING** — There are reminders of the real, physical pain that the soldiers experience, as well as their exhaustion and fatigue. Even thinking about home is painful for the men as they're not welcome there.
2) **BOREDOM** — There's a sense of frustration at their situation — they are "Worried", "Watching" and waiting, but "nothing happens" and the men are left to contemplate their own deaths.
3) **HOPELESSNESS** — The soldiers are helpless against the power of nature and there is nothing they can do to change their situation. The poem offers little hope of a future for the men.

Go a step further and give a personal response

Have a go at answering these questions to help you come up with your own ideas about the poem:

Q1. What do you think the title is referring to? Could it have more than one meaning?

Q2. Do you think the men are relieved about a new day dawning? How can you tell?

Q3. Why do you think the word "ghosts" is used to describe the men thinking about going home?

Reality of war, power of nature, loss and absence...

The reality of war is also a key theme in 'Charge of the Light Brigade' and 'Bayonet Charge', while 'Storm on the Island' focuses on the power of nature. 'London' is another poem with a total absence of hope.

Storm on the Island

This is a very strong opening statement that creates a feeling of safety. Compare it to the last line of the poem.

The island seems barren — nothing grows there.

The plosive sound has a greater impact because it comes at the start of the line.

In a Greek tragedy, a "chorus" comments on and explains events. Having no trees to act as a chorus suggests the islanders are left on their own to face and interpret the storm.

Caesura slows the pace of the line and emphasises the second "no".

Oxymoron juxtaposes the feelings of fear and safety.

This is language normally used to describe war. The wind is compared to a fighter plane attacking the island.

We are prepared: we build our houses squat,
Sink walls in rock and roof them with good slate.
This wizened earth has never troubled us
With hay, so, as you can see, there are no stacks
5 Or stooks that can be lost. Nor are there trees
Which might prove company when it blows full
Blast: you know what I mean – leaves and branches
Can raise a tragic chorus in a gale
So that you can listen to the thing you fear
10 Forgetting that it pummels your house too.
But there are no trees, no natural shelter.
You might think that the sea is company,
Exploding comfortably down on the cliffs
But no: when it begins, the flung spray hits
15 The very windows, spits like a tame cat
Turned savage. We just sit tight while wind dives
And strafes invisibly. Space is a salvo.
We are bombarded by the empty air.
Strange, it is a huge nothing that we fear.

There are lots of words about safety and security in the first two lines. The end-stopping reinforces this feeling of security, which disappears with the enjambment in the rest of the poem.

The word "company" is used here and on line 12, to emphasise the loneliness of the setting.

The narrator speaks directly to the reader in a chatty tone, making you reflect on your own experience of storms.

This is a very violent verb to describe the wind.

This simile shows how familiar things become frightening during the storm.

The assonant 'i' sounds and sibilant sounds in lines 14-17 combine to imitate the hissing and spitting of the sea.

The storm is invisible — there's nothing solid there. This contrasts with the solid rock mentioned in the second line of the poem.

<u>Context — Northern Ireland</u>
The first eight letters of the poem's title spell 'Stormont'. 'Stormont' is the name given to Northern Ireland's parliament buildings. This hints that the 'storm' could be about some of the violent political disturbances that Ireland has experienced, e.g. between Catholics and Protestants, or Irish republicans wanting independence from Britain.

<u>POEM DICTIONARY</u>
wizened — dried up
stooks — bundles of a crop stacked together and left in a field to dry
strafe — to rake with gunfire at close range, often from the air
salvo — lots of guns firing at once

Seamus Heaney

Seamus Heaney was a Northern Irish poet who won the Nobel Prize for Literature in 1995 and died in 2013. He often wrote about themes such as childhood, nature and his homeland. This poem was published in 1966.

You've got to know what the poem's about

1) The narrator describes how a community thinks it's well-prepared for a coming storm.
2) As the poem goes on, their confidence starts to disappear as the storm develops. The power and the sounds of the storm are described.
3) The ending of the poem describes the fear as the storm hits the island.

Learn about the form, structure and language

1) **FORM** — The poem is written in blank verse, which mirrors the patterns of everyday speech and makes the poem sound like part of a conversation. The first person plural ("We") is used, showing how this is a collective, communal experience. The poem is all in one stanza — it's compact and sturdy, like the houses.
2) **STRUCTURE** — The poem shifts from security to fear. "But no:" seems to be a turning point (volta), with the slow pace of the monosyllabic phrase and the caesura reflecting the last moments of calm before the storm.
3) **CONTRASTING DESCRIPTIONS OF SAFETY AND FEAR** — The narrator uses a lot of words to do with safety and security at the beginning of the poem. The tone changes though, and the sense of danger increases as familiar things become frightening during the storm.
4) **DIRECT ADDRESS** — The narrator involves the reader in his fear by speaking directly to "you".
5) **VIOLENT IMAGERY** — The storm is described in violent, often warlike terms, with similes, metaphors and personification combining to emphasise the danger and effects of the storm.
6) **USE OF SOUNDS** — Forceful sounds (e.g. "Blast") are used to demonstrate the strength of nature, and the poem also uses assonant and sibilant sounds to reflect the noise of the wind and waves.

Remember the feelings and attitudes in the poem

1) **SAFETY** — The first part of the poem shows that the community feels safe, and prepared for the storm.
2) **FEAR** — This sense of security soon changes to fear, as familiar things change and become frightening.
3) **HELPLESSNESS** — The people can't do anything about their fear except wait for the storm to finish. Nature is presented as a powerful, relentless force.

Steve saw the storm as the perfect opportunity to try out his new kite.

Go a step further and give a personal response

Have a go at answering these questions to help you come up with your own ideas about the poem:

Q1.	Do you think the speaker likes living on the island? Why / why not?
Q2.	What's the effect of describing the "leaves and branches" as a "tragic chorus"?
Q3.	Why do you think the poem addresses the reader directly? What effect does it have on you?
Q4.	What is the effect of comparing the sea to a "tame cat / Turned savage"?

Power of nature, fear, individual experiences of place...

If you're writing about fear or the power of nature, look at 'Bayonet Charge' or 'The Prelude'. You could consider how feelings for a place are presented in this poem compared with 'The Emigrée' or 'London'.

Bayonet Charge

Sounds as if he's in a confused, vulnerable state. The events seem like a nightmare, but this confirms that they're real.

This has a double meaning — it suggests discomfort but also inexperience.

Violent imagery and onomatopoeia describes the sound and impact of the shots.

The repeated 'h' sound imitates the soldier's heavy breathing as he runs.

Suddenly he awoke and was running – raw
In raw-seamed hot khaki, his sweat heavy,
Stumbling across a field of clods towards a green hedge
That dazzled with rifle fire, hearing
5 Bullets smacking the belly out of the air –
He lugged a rifle numb as a smashed arm;
The patriotic tear that had brimmed in his eye
Sweating like molten iron from the centre of his chest, –

His patriotism has turned to fear and pain — his heroic ideals have been replaced by painful reality.

Simile suggests his rifle is useless and foreshadows the injuries he's likely to get.

This stanza pauses the action and focuses on the soldier wondering why he is there.

Emphasises the soldier's insignificance and his lack of control of his situation. "cold" implies that the people in charge of the war don't care about individual soldiers.

In bewilderment then he almost stopped –
10 In what cold clockwork of the stars and the nations
Was he the hand pointing that second? He was running
Like a man who has jumped up in the dark and runs
Listening between his footfalls for the reason
Of his still running, and his foot hung like
15 Statuary in mid-stride. Then the shot-slashed furrows

Simile creates an image of someone blind and irrational — suggests there's no rational reason for war.

The caesura ends his period of thought and forces him to return to reality.

It's as if the soldier is turned to stone by his bewilderment.

A distressing image of out-of-control movement. "threshing circle" is an agricultural term, used to suggest that nature is affected by war.

Threw up a yellow hare that rolled like a flame
And crawled in a threshing circle, its mouth wide
Open silent, its eyes standing out.
He plunged past with his bayonet toward the green hedge,
20 King, honour, human dignity, etcetera
Dropped like luxuries in a yelling alarm
To get out of that blue crackling air
His terror's touchy dynamite.

Simile emphasises the hare's frantic movement and hints at the danger the soldier is in.

Suggests pain and fear beyond expression.

Natural image contrasts with the violence and terror of war.

He's been reduced to a basic level — he's attacking out of desperation, not moral principle.

These are the reasons that persuade people to go to war. Using "etcetera" suggests they're not even worth listing.

The soldier seems to have become a weapon rather than a human being. He's driven purely by his terror.

Context — World War One
Although it was written much later, the poem is set during World War One. It describes a soldier going 'over the top' — this was when soldiers climbed out of their trenches and charged towards enemy lines, carrying their bayonets. These charges usually resulted in heavy casualties.

POEM DICTIONARY
bayonet — a blade / knife that's attached to the end of a rifle
clods — lumps of earth
statuary — a group of statues
threshing — thrashing, or the beating of crops (e.g. corn) to separate the crop from the straw

Ted Hughes

Ted Hughes was a 20th-century English poet. His father served in and survived World War One, and Ted spent two years as a mechanic in the RAF before going to university. 'Bayonet Charge' was published in 1957.

You've got to know what the poem's about

1) The poem focuses on a single soldier's experience of a charge towards enemy lines. It describes his thoughts and actions as he tries to stay alive.
2) The soldier's overriding emotion and motivation is fear, which has replaced the more patriotic ideals that he held before the violence began.

Learn about the form, structure and language

1) **FORM** — The poem uses enjambment and caesura, and has lines of uneven length. This creates an irregular rhythm, which mirrors the soldier struggling to run through the mud. The narrator uses the pronoun "he" rather than naming the soldier to keep him anonymous. It suggests that he is a universal figure who could represent any young soldier.
2) **STRUCTURE** — The poem starts *in medias res* (in the middle of the action) and covers the soldier's movements and thoughts over a short space of time. The first stanza sees the soldier acting on instinct, but time seems to stand still in the second stanza, when the soldier begins to think about his situation. In the final stanza, he gives up his thoughts and ideals and seems to have lost his humanity.
3) **VIOLENT IMAGERY** — There is some shocking imagery which brings home the sights and sounds of war. This helps to strongly convey the sense of confusion and fear.
4) **FIGURATIVE LANGUAGE** — The poem includes powerful figurative language to emphasise the horror and physical pain of the charge, and also to question the point of war.
5) **NATURAL IMAGERY** — The repeated references to the "green hedge" and the mention of a "field" and "threshing circle" show the natural, agricultural setting of the war. The painful image of the "yellow hare" reminds the reader of how the natural world is also damaged by war.

Remember the feelings and attitudes in the poem

1) **TERROR** — The poem challenges patriotism and shows how desperate terror becomes the overriding emotion in battle. The soldier is driven forward by fear rather than any more noble motive.
2) **CONFUSION** — The soldier is physically disorientated by the gunfire, but he's also questioning what he's doing there at all.

Dress sense, self-respect, human dignity etcetera dropped like luxuries.

Go a step further and give a personal response

Have a go at answering these questions to help you come up with your own ideas about the poem:

Q1. How does the middle stanza differ from the other two stanzas?

Q2. How does the speaker show the soldier changing between the start and the end of the poem?

Q3. How is natural imagery used in the poem to emphasise the horror of the soldier's situation?

Q4. What does the poem suggest about the poet's attitude to war?

Effects of conflict, reality of war, fear...

This poem examines the deadly effects and realities of war — 'Exposure' and 'The Charge of the Light Brigade' do similar things. You could also compare the soldier's fear with that of the narrator in 'The Prelude'.

Remains

This sounds like one in a series of stories, and the reader is listening in.

On another occasion, we get sent out
to tackle looters raiding a bank.
And one of them legs it up the road,
probably armed, possibly not.

Colloquial expression — makes it sound like an ordinary anecdote.

There's doubt here, which contrasts strongly with the definite action that follows.

Repetition sounds like he's keen for the reader to know it wasn't just him — hints that he feels guilty.

5 Well myself and somebody else and somebody else
are all of the same mind,
so all three of us open fire.
Three of a kind all letting fly, and I swear

This comes as a surprise — the sudden violence doesn't fit with the casual tone.

Poetic voice switches to "I" — this is now more personal.

This violent metaphor contrasts shockingly with the colloquial style of the first two stanzas.

I see every round as it rips through his life –
10 I see broad daylight on the other side.
So we've hit this looter a dozen times
and he's there on the ground, sort of inside out,

This is quite a grotesque, exaggerated image — he says he can see straight through the bullet holes in the man's body.

Repetition of "I see" emphasises the visual horror of the scene.

This is an almost childish description of the man's body — the speaker seems unable to process it in an adult way.

pain itself, the image of agony.
One of my mates goes by
15 and tosses his guts back into his body.
Then he's carted off in the back of a lorry.

Two very casual, cold actions — no respect for the dead man. "tosses" and "carted off" make it sound as if the body is a piece of rubbish.

Turning point (volta) in the poem. The speaker's mood changes.

End of story, except not really.
His blood-shadow stays on the street, and out on patrol
I walk right over it week after week.
20 Then I'm home on leave. But I blink

A visual reminder of the death — it foreshadows the memories that are going to haunt him.

Short, simple sentence suggests he thinks that once he's at home he'll forget the terrible things he's seen. The suddenness of the line also hints at the speaker being confused.

The stanza ending reflects the blinking — the enjambment carries you forwards, and the horror is still there when the next stanza starts.

and he bursts again through the doors of the bank.
Sleep, and he's probably armed, possibly not.
Dream, and he's torn apart by a dozen rounds.
And the drink and the drugs won't flush him out –

Short words, separated from the rest of the line by caesurae, sound like gun shots.

Repetition of line 4 shows that he's replaying the event in his mind, and hints at his inner turmoil.

25 he's here in my head when I close my eyes,
dug in behind enemy lines,
not left for dead in some distant, sun-stunned, sand-smothered land
or six-feet-under in desert sand,

The metaphor compares the memory stuck in his mind to a soldier in a trench.

The violent parts of the compound adjectives, "stunned" and "smothered", show how the place is affected by war. The long line and the sibilance slow the pace and reflect the speaker's lack of clear thought.

but near to the knuckle, here and now,
30 his bloody life in my bloody hands.

There could be a double meaning to "bloody" — he's talking about the man's blood, but also swearing in anger.

There's no collective responsibility now — he feels completely responsible.

Possible reference to *Macbeth* — after persuading her husband to kill King Duncan, Lady Macbeth sleepwalks and tries to wash imaginary blood from her hands. This allusion hints that the speaker has been unbalanced by his guilt, as Lady Macbeth was.

Simon Armitage

Armitage is an English poet, playwright and novelist. 'Remains' is from his 2008 collection, *The Not Dead*, which looks at the effect of war on ex-soldiers. It's based on the account of a British soldier who served in Iraq.

You've got to know what the poem's about

Josh was appointed lookout to make sure there'd be no raids on this bank.

1) A group of soldiers shoot a man who's running away from a bank raid he's been involved in. His death is described in graphic detail.
2) The soldier telling the story isn't sure whether the man was armed or not — this plays on his mind.
3) He can't get the man's death out of his head — he's haunted by it.

Learn about the form, structure and language

1) **FORM** — There's no regular line length or rhyme scheme, making it sound like someone telling a story. The speaker starts with the first person plural ("we"), but changes to first person singular ("I") and the poem becomes more personal, sounding like a confession. In the final couplet, both lines have the same metre — this gives a feeling of finality and hints that the guilt will stay with the soldier.
2) **STRUCTURE** — The poem begins as if it's going to be an amusing anecdote, but it quickly turns into a graphic description of a man's death. There is a clear volta (turning point) at the beginning of the fifth stanza, where the soldier's tone, thoughts and emotions are changed by his guilt.
3) **GRAPHIC IMAGERY** — The man's death is described in gory detail, with the implication that his "guts" have spilt out onto the ground. The imagery reminds the reader of the horrors of war, but also shows how desensitised to violence and death the speaker was at the time — they had become part of his everyday life.
4) **COLLOQUIAL LANGUAGE** — The first four stanzas have lots of chatty, familiar language, which helps make the poem sound like someone telling a story. However, this language also trivialises the man's death.
5) **REPETITION** — Words are repeated to reflect the way that the killing is repeated in the speaker's mind.

Remember the feelings and attitudes in the poem

1) **NONCHALANCE** — Initially, there's a very casual attitude towards the death of the man — the tone at the start of the poem is anecdotal. He's shot without warning and his body is just thrown into a lorry and "carted off".
2) **GUILT** — The speaker can't get the memory of the killing out of his mind. He is tormented by thoughts of the man, and wondering whether he was armed or not. The poem ends with the speaker acknowledging that he has blood on his hands — he knows he's guilty.

Go a step further and give a personal response

Have a go at answering these questions to help you come up with your own ideas about the poem:

Q1. Why do you think Armitage chose the title he did? Do you think it's an effective title?

Q2. In anecdotes you usually use people's names. Why does the speaker just say "somebody else"?

Q3. Why do you think the word "flush" is used in line 24?

Q4. What does the phrase "near to the knuckle" suggest about how the death is affecting the speaker?

Memory, effects of conflict, individual experiences...

You could compare the importance of memory in this poem and 'Kamikaze'. 'Poppies', 'Bayonet Charge' and 'War Photographer' all explore individual experiences of war and the effects of conflict.

Poppies

Three days before Armistice Sunday
and poppies had already been placed
on individual war graves. Before you left,
I pinned one onto your lapel, crimped petals,
5 spasms of paper red, disrupting a blockade
of yellow bias binding around your blazer.

Sellotape bandaged around my hand,
I rounded up as many white cat hairs
as I could, smoothed down your shirt's
10 upturned collar, steeled the softening
of my face. I wanted to graze my nose
across the tip of your nose, play at
being Eskimos like we did when
you were little. I resisted the impulse
15 to run my fingers through the gelled
blackthorns of your hair. All my words
flattened, rolled, turned into felt,

slowly melting. I was brave, as I walked
with you, to the front door, threw
20 it open, the world overflowing
like a treasure chest. A split second
and you were away, intoxicated.
After you'd gone I went into your bedroom,
released a song bird from its cage.
25 Later a single dove flew from the pear tree,
and this is where it has led me,
skirting the church yard walls, my stomach busy
making tucks, darts, pleats, hat-less, without
a winter coat or reinforcements of scarf, gloves.

30 On reaching the top of the hill I traced
the inscriptions on the war memorial,
leaned against it like a wishbone.
The dove pulled freely against the sky,
an ornamental stitch. I listened, hoping to hear
35 your playground voice catching on the wind.

An ominous reminder that war kills individuals, so loss is personal.

Repetition emphasises the parallel between national and personal mourning and remembrance.

Suggests that she feels shut out from her son's life.

Makes the reader think of an injured body.

Another image of being wounded. She is emotionally wounded and he might be wounded in war.

Domestic, motherly image — this may be the last time she can do this for her son.

Alliteration emphasises she's trying to be brave and not show emotion.

Caesurae reflect the mother's attempt to stay in control — she doesn't want to get carried away with her emotions.

This reference to the sense of touch shows how the mother longs for the closeness she had with her son when he was small, and emphasises the distance between them now.

The "blackthorns" allude to Jesus, who wore a crown of thorns when he was crucified. This hints at the sacrifice the son may make.

"felt" suggests she speaks softly and aligns her with domesticity.

The mother's composure briefly disappears, as shown by the "melting" of her words.

The mother asserting her bravery here subverts the idea that it's only those who go off to war who are brave.

Sudden movement suggests breaking a boundary.

Simile shows the world from the son's perspective — makes it sound exciting and full of precious experiences.

The son's excitement contrasts with his mother's sadness. However, "intoxicated" also hints at a lack of control — the son's giving up control of his life by joining the army.

Symbolises her son leaving.

Doves are a symbol of peace but also of mourning.

Sewing imagery conveys her nervousness and physical feelings of anxiety.

Battle imagery makes her sound vulnerable.

Touch is important to the mother — the memorial is a solid object, unlike her wishes and memories.

A reminder of the risks her son faces.

Strong visual image hints at her wish for his safety.

Strong visual image of something small and beautiful in a vast space — represents her son.

Alliteration echoes the way she's straining to hear him.

Links leaving to join the army with leaving to go to school.

POEM DICTIONARY

Armistice — an agreement to end fighting. The armistice signed at the end of World War One, along with the people who died in the conflict, are remembered in November each year.

bias binding — a strip of fabric sewn on to conceal rough edges or add decoration. It could indicate the son's rank or regiment here.

Jane Weir

Jane Weir is a writer and textile designer who grew up in Manchester and Italy, and has also lived in Belfast. 'Poppies' was one of a collection of 21st-century war poems commissioned in 2009 by Carol Ann Duffy.

You've got to know what the poem's about

1) A mother describes her son leaving home, seemingly to join the army.
2) The poem is about the mother's emotional reaction to her son leaving — she feels sad, lonely and scared for his safety.
3) She describes helping him smarten his uniform ready to leave. After he leaves, she goes to places that remind her of him, desperately trying to find any trace of him.

Learn about the form, structure and language

1) **FORM** — The first-person narrative means that the reader gets a strong impression of the mother's emotions. There is no regular rhyme or rhythm, which makes it sound like the narrator's thoughts and memories. Long sentences and enjambment give the impression that the narrator is absorbed in her own thoughts and memories, whilst caesurae show how she tries to hold her emotions together.
2) **STRUCTURE** — The poem is chronological, describing preparations for the son leaving, his departure and then what the mother does afterwards. However, the time frame is ambiguous — memories of the son's childhood are intermingled with memories of him leaving, and they're often not clearly distinguished.
3) **USE OF THE SENSES** — The mother's separation from her son is emphasised by the way she can't touch or hear him. She touches other things and listens for his voice "on the wind", but this can't replace her son.
4) **WAR IMAGERY** — Images of war and violence symbolise the son's new identity and the danger that he's in. References to "Armistice Sunday" and the "war memorial" make the reader question whether he is still alive.
5) **DOMESTIC IMAGERY** — The images of war are mixed with poignant images of home and family life.

Remember the feelings and attitudes in the poem

1) **LOSS** — The mother acts as if she's lost her son — she is struggling to move on and accept the changes. There are hints that the son may even be dead. References to the son starting school allude to a different kind of loss that the mother has previously experienced.
2) **FEAR** — The mother is anxious and fearful for her son's safety. Her anxiety has a physical effect on her. The poem focuses on the bravery and restraint of the people left behind when their loved ones go to war.
3) **FREEDOM** — The poem shows the contrasting perspectives between the loss the mother feels and the freedom and excitement her son experiences.

Go a step further and give a personal response

Have a go at answering these questions to help you come up with your own ideas about the poem:

Q1. Is this a poem about war or a poem about family? Explain your answer.

Q2. What impression do you get of the mother through the things that she does?

Q3. Do you think the son is still alive? What clues does the poem give you?

Q4. How do you think the title relates to the poem?

Effects of conflict, loss and absence, identity...

Effects of conflict are covered in several poems, including 'War Photographer'. You could compare family identity here with national identity in 'Kamikaze', or look at loss in this poem and 'The Emigrée'.

War Photographer

In his darkroom he is finally alone
with spools of suffering set out in ordered rows.
The only light is red and softly glows,
as though this were a church and he
5 a priest preparing to intone a Mass.
Belfast. Beirut. Phnom Penh. All flesh is grass.

He has a job to do. Solutions slop in trays
beneath his hands, which did not tremble then
though seem to now. Rural England. Home again
10 to ordinary pain which simple weather can dispel,
to fields which don't explode beneath the feet
of running children in a nightmare heat.

Something is happening. A stranger's features
faintly start to twist before his eyes,
15 a half-formed ghost. He remembers the cries
of this man's wife, how he sought approval
without words to do what someone must
and how the blood stained into foreign dust.

A hundred agonies in black and white
20 from which his editor will pick out five or six
for Sunday's supplement. The reader's eyeballs prick
with tears between the bath and pre-lunch beers.
From the aeroplane he stares impassively at where
he earns his living and they do not care.

The phrase tells us where he is, but "dark" also hints at the subject matter of his photographs.

The reels of film are described like soldiers, or like rows of war graves. Paradox — chaos and suffering are reduced to something ordered.

This simile shows the seriousness of his work. This is a solemn act, almost like a funeral mass.

The succession of plosive sounds breaks the soft mood like gunfire.

This is a quote from the Bible (Isaiah 40:6) which means that human life is temporary.

Short, simple sentence using monosyllabic words — he has to put his emotions aside, like a soldier does.

Irony — he was calm in the face of horrors, but now they affect him.

May be a reference to a Vietnam War photo (see below). The link hints at the importance of the photographer's work, as the photo is sometimes credited with helping to end the war.

Soft sounds contrast strongly with the place names in stanza one.

Turning point (volta) in the poem. The focus switches to the personal cost of war — he's remembering a specific death and its impact.

Focusing on one photo and family makes this personal and emphasises the real suffering of war.

He's "half-formed" because the photograph is still developing, but also suggests his body's been mutilated.

Emphasises that he has an important role in informing the public of the reality of war.

Emotive metaphor to describe his photos. Having the pictures printed seems to confirm and solidify the suffering they show.

Reminder that this is all happening somewhere else. "stained" hints at the lasting impact of war.

The sibilant and plosive sounds make the reader almost spit the words out. This may hint at frustration that the photos aren't considered important enough to feature in the main newspaper.

"prick" suggests pain, but only a small amount of pain for a short time. This suggests the readers will quickly forget the photos.

The internal rhyme of "tears" and "beers" emphasises the short duration of the readers' pain — the tears will quickly be replaced with beers.

Suggestion that he's returning to the war zone — like a soldier, he's been home on leave, but now must return to do his job.

This is ambiguous — it could refer to the readers of the newspapers who don't care about the victims of war, or it could refer to the wider world, which is apathetic about others' suffering.

Context — Nick Ut's 'Napalm Girl' photo

The imagery in line 12 seems to reference a famous photo by another war photographer, Nick Ut. He took a photo of a nine-year-old Vietnamese girl, Kim Phúc, during the Vietnam War. The photo shows Kim Phúc running naked towards the camera in extreme pain — she'd torn her clothes off after being severely burned when her village was hit by a napalm bomb (a bomb designed to start fires). The photo was published on the front page of the New York Times and won a Pulitzer Prize.

POEM DICTIONARY

intone — recite or sing a prayer or chant
Beirut — the capital of Lebanon in the Middle East
Phnom Penh — the capital of Cambodia in South-East Asia
dispel — get rid of
Sunday's supplement — the magazine which comes with the Sunday newspaper

Carol Ann Duffy

Carol Ann Duffy is a Scottish poet who, in 2009, became the first woman to hold the post of Poet Laureate. 'War Photographer' was published in 1985 as part of Duffy's collection, *Standing Female Nude*.

You've got to know what the poem's about

1) A war photographer is in his darkroom, developing pictures that he's taken in war zones across the world. Being back in England is a big contrast — it's safe and calm compared to where he's been.
2) A photo begins to develop, and the photographer remembers the death of the man, and the cries of his wife.
3) The final stanza focuses on the people in England who will see his photographs in their Sunday papers. The speaker thinks that they don't really care about the people and places in the photographs.

Learn about the form, structure and language

1) **FORM** — The poem has four stanzas of equal length and a regular rhyme scheme — it is "set out in ordered rows" like the photographer's spools, echoing the care that the photographer takes over his work. The use of enjambment reflects the gradual revealing of the photo as it develops.
2) **STRUCTURE** — The poem follows the actions and thoughts of the photographer in his darkroom. There's a distinct change at the start of the third stanza, when the photographer remembers a specific death. In the final stanza, the focus shifts to the way the photographer's work is received.
3) **RELIGIOUS IMAGERY** — The references to religion make it sound almost as if the photographer is a priest conducting a funeral when he's developing the photos — there's a sense of ceremony to his actions.
4) **CONTRASTS** — The poem presents "Rural England" as a contrast to the war zones the photographer visits. The grieving widow is compared with people in England whose eyes only "prick / with tears" at the pain. Ironically, the photographer is detached in the war zones but deeply affected at home.
5) **EMOTIVE LANGUAGE** — The poem is full of powerful, emotive imagery which reflects the horrors of war seen by the photographer and captured in his photos. Like the photographer, Duffy tries to represent the true horror of conflict in her work in order to make the reader think about the subject.

Remember the feelings and attitudes in the poem

1) **PAIN** — The photographs depict real pain ("A hundred agonies") and there's also the emotional pain of the woman who's lost her husband. The horrific pain of war is contrasted with the "ordinary" pain back home.
2) **DETACHMENT** — The photographer is detached from his emotions in the war zones so he can do his job. The words "finally alone" and "impassively" suggest that he's also detached from "ordinary" life in England.
3) **ANGER** — The poem ends with a sense of anger at the people who don't care about the suffering of others.

Go a step further and give a personal response

Have a go at answering these questions to help you come up with your own ideas about the poem:

Q1. Why do you think the photographer's hands tremble when he's developing the photos?

Q2. Do you think the photographer enjoys being back in England? Explain your answer.

Q3. Describe the mood in the final stanza of the poem.

Q4. Do you think Duffy admires the photographer? Why / why not?

Memory, individual experiences, effects of conflict...

The effect of the photographer's memories in this poem could be compared with those of the soldier in 'Remains'. 'Bayonet Charge' and 'Kamikaze' offer contrasting experiences of conflict and its effects.

Tissue

Paper that lets the light
shine through, this
is what could alter things.
Paper thinned by age or touching,

"Paper" begins the first two sentences in the poem, drawing the reader's attention. This suggests that it's important and can perhaps drive the change that the third line alludes to.

Light allows things to be seen, rather than hidden. This may hint at what needs to change.

5 the kind you find in well-used books,
the back of the Koran, where a hand
has written in the names and histories,
who was born to whom,

Mentioning the Koran broadens the importance of paper — it can be used to record beliefs.

Paper is used to record family history — whole lives can be summed up by marks on paper.

the height and weight, who
10 died where and how, on which sepia date,
pages smoothed and stroked and turned
transparent with attention.

Gentle verbs and repetition of "and" shows that the pages are treated with respect and affection — the description makes them sound almost as if they're a child or a pet.

Having "attention" as the last word before the first full stop emphasises the importance of what's come before.

If buildings were paper, I might
feel their drift, see how easily
15 they fall away on a sigh, a shift
in the direction of the wind.

There's a shift in tone here. The speaker suggests that if buildings were made out of paper, people would notice that they are only temporary.

Rhyming "shift" and "drift" plays on the idea of movement — they appear in different places on the line as if they've been blown by the wind.

Maps too. The sun shines through
their borderlines, the marks
that rivers make, roads,
20 railtracks, mountainfolds,

A short, blunt sentence, which may reflect the fixed nature of maps and borders — they create division rather than freedom.

The sun is a powerful, permanent force, whereas borders are just temporary marks on paper.

The alliteration creates a flowing effect and a sense of freedom.

Fine slips from grocery shops
that say how much was sold
and what was paid by credit card
might fly our lives like paper kites.

Receipts record our day-to-day lives. They can tell a story about our whole existence.

The simile hints at how our lives can be controlled by money.

25 An architect could use all this,
place layer over layer, luminous
script over numbers over line,
and never wish to build again with brick

The work of the poet mirrors the work of the architect — the poet builds layers of words and meanings, where an architect designs physical structures. The repetition of "over" reinforces the idea of layers.

The consonance of "brick" and "block" emphasises the solidity of the objects, and the enjambment gives the words more impact.

or block, but let the daylight break
30 through capitals and monoliths,
through the shapes that pride can make,
find a way to trace a grand design

These lines repeat the image in lines 17 and 18. Light is enduring and powerful — it will continue to shine even when man-made structures break.

This sounds like a criticism of human pride — we create big, imposing buildings that are ultimately unimportant.

There's a shift from talking about paper to talking about humans — a construction more complex and more "grand" than any building.

with living tissue, raise a structure
never meant to last,
35 of paper smoothed and stroked
and thinned to be transparent,

Human life is only temporary, but the repetition of line 11 reminds us that we're all part of a complex, lasting family history.

turned into your skin.

The references to creation in the previous two stanzas suggest that this could be addressed to a child. It could also be addressed to the reader, reminding us that we're all influenced by our heritage.

POEM DICTIONARY
Koran (or Qur'an) — the holy book of Islam
sepia — a brownish-grey colour
monoliths — large stone statues or columns

Imtiaz Dharker

Imtiaz Dharker was born in Pakistan, raised in Glasgow and now lives in Britain and India. 'Tissue' is from her 2006 collection, *The Terrorist at My Table* — the collection questions how well we know the people around us.

You've got to know what the poem's about

The poem resists a straightforward interpretation, but there are some key themes and ideas:

1) The first three stanzas talk about the importance of paper as a means of recording our history.
2) Stanzas four to six focus on the paradox that paper is fragile, yet it still controls our lives.
3) The final thirteen lines look at creating things, particularly human life. Life is more complex and precious than other things we create. It's also temporary, but forms part of a bigger and ongoing story.

Learn about the form, structure and language

1) **FORM** — The poetic voice is elusive, with the focus on humanity in general rather than a specific person or speaker. The lack of regular rhythm or rhyme and the enjambment across lines and stanzas gives the poem a freedom and openness, reflecting the narrator's desire for freedom and clarity. The short stanzas mean that the poem is built up in layers, just as it suggests human life is.
2) **STRUCTURE** — There are three main parts to the poem, moving through ideas about history, human experience and the creation of human life. The final, single line stands out and focuses the reader on their own identity and how it's created.
3) **LANGUAGE ABOUT LIGHT** — Light is presented as a positive force — it enables people to see and understand, it can move through and beyond boundaries and it can break through objects.
4) **LANGUAGE ABOUT CREATION** — There are lots of references to things being created. Man-made constructions like buildings and borderlines are compared with the creation of humans.
5) **DIFFERENT TYPES OF TISSUE** — The homonyms of 'tissue' create a link between paper and humans — both tissue paper and human tissue are fragile, but powerful. The word 'tissue' originally meant something that had been woven, which reinforces the idea that human lives are built up in layers.

Remember the feelings and attitudes in the poem

1) **CONTROL** — The poem mentions different things that control human life — there are references to money, religion, nature, pride and governments ("capitals").
2) **FREEDOM** — The speaker imagines a world that breaks free of some of these restrictions, where human constructions are less permanent and important.

Go a step further and give a personal response

Have a go at answering these questions to help you come up with your own ideas about the poem:

Q1. Why do you think the poet lists details of what families might write in the back of the Koran?

Q2. The word "transparent" is repeated on lines 12 and 36. Why do you think this is?

Q3. Why do you think the architect would "never wish to build again with brick"?

Q4. Why does Dharker describe the human body as a "structure"?

Power of nature, power of humans, identity...

'Ozymandias' is another poem that looks at how nature is ultimately more powerful than human power or achievements. The importance of family identity is a common feature of this poem and 'Poppies'.

The Emigrée

There once was a country... I left it as a child
but my memory of it is sunlight-clear
for it seems I never saw it in that November
which, I am told, comes to the mildest city.
5 The worst news I receive of it cannot break
my original view, the bright, filled paperweight.
It may be at war, it may be sick with tyrants,
but I am branded by an impression of sunlight.

The white streets of that city, the graceful slopes
10 glow even clearer as time rolls its tanks
and the frontiers rise between us, close like waves.
That child's vocabulary I carried here
like a hollow doll, opens and spills a grammar.
Soon I shall have every coloured molecule of it.
15 It may by now be a lie, banned by the state
but I can't get it off my tongue. It tastes of sunlight.

I have no passport, there's no way back at all
but my city comes to me in its own white plane.
It lies down in front of me, docile as paper;
20 I comb its hair and love its shining eyes.
My city takes me dancing through the city
of walls. They accuse me of absence, they circle me.
They accuse me of being dark in their free city.
My city hides behind me. They mutter death,
25 and my shadow falls as evidence of sunlight.

The opening makes it sound like a story, but it also suggests loss.

This suggests that the memory is clear and happy.

This hints at another voice telling her about her past.

"November" represents difficult times, when things are cold, dark and gloomy.

Metaphor suggests that the narrator's memories are bright and positive, but also solid and fixed.

The negative "branded" is juxtaposed with the positive "impression of sunlight". "branded" also suggests a permanence to her view — it can't change.

Suggestion that the country has been invaded and that the speaker's positive view of it isn't accurate.

The description makes the "city" sound pure, almost heavenly.

Time is personified as an enemy, but it can't affect the speaker's memories.

This seems to refer to the language of her childhood — the metaphor makes the language seem bright and precious.

Using another sense (taste) increases the vividness of the experience.

The first line of the stanza sounds hopeless, but the next line changes the mood again.

The city is personified — the "white plane" could represent the speaker's memories.

There's a childlike joy in this description — it sounds like a child playing with a pet.

Contrasting perceptions of the city the speaker is now in — she sees it as restrictive, but "they" see it as "free".

It's unclear who "They" are, but they are menacing, and the repetition reinforces their threat to the speaker.

The speaker is accused of being "dark" in her current city — this contrasts with the brightness she associates with her old city.

The poem ends on a positive note — despite the threats of death, the city is still associated with "sunlight", just as it is at the end of the first two stanzas.

"Who are you calling 'hollow'?"

POEM DICTIONARY
emigrée — a woman forced to leave her native country, often for political reasons

Carol Rumens

Carol Rumens is an English poet, lecturer and translator. She has published over fifteen collections of poetry, as well as several novels and plays. 'The Emigrée' appeared in her 1993 collection, *Thinking of Skins*.

You've got to know what the poem's about

1) The speaker talks about a city in a country she left as a child — she has a purely positive view of it.
2) The city seems to be under attack and unreachable, but in the third stanza it appears to the speaker. An unknown "They" accuse and threaten the speaker, but she still sees the old city in a positive way.
3) The city may not be a real place — it could represent a time, person or emotion that the speaker has been forced to leave.

Learn about the form, structure and language

1) **FORM** — The poem is written in the first person, with three eight-line stanzas but no regular rhythm or rhyme scheme. The first two stanzas contain lots of enjambment, but there's more end-stopping in the final stanza. This reflects the speaker's feeling of confinement in her new "city of walls".
2) **STRUCTURE** — The speaker's memory of the city grows and solidifies as the poem moves on — the city becomes a physical presence for the speaker in the final stanza. Each stanza ends with "sunlight", reinforcing the fact that the speaker sees the city in a positive light.
3) **LANGUAGE OF CONFLICT** — Vocabulary associated with war, invasion and tyranny shows that the city may not be as perfect as the speaker remembers it. In the second stanza, there's the sense that the speaker is defying the authorities by accessing her "child's vocabulary" that's been "banned".
4) **LANGUAGE ABOUT LIGHT** — The city is described in bright, colourful terms, emphasising the speaker's feeling that it's a beautiful, positive place. The repeated link with "sunlight" suggests a vitality to the city.
5) **PERSONIFICATION** — The city is initially personified as being "sick with tyrants". In the final stanza, it appears to the speaker, lies down and then later takes her dancing. Describing the city in human terms emphasises the strength of the speaker's love for it.

Remember the feelings and attitudes in the poem

1) **NOSTALGIA** — The speaker's positive memories of the city are unwavering — nothing she hears will change her view of it. There's a sense of yearning for the city and the past, which is partly fulfilled by the city appearing to the speaker in the final stanza.
2) **THREAT** — There are suggestions that the city has been invaded or taken over by a tyrant, but the speaker chooses to ignore these things. She is threatened in her new city, and seems to have to protect her old city. The poem ends with "sunlight", but this doesn't entirely remove the sense of threat.

Go a step further and give a personal response

Have a go at answering these questions to help you come up with your own ideas about the poem:

Q1. What does the title of the poem suggest about how the speaker feels about leaving the city?
Q2. Why does Rumens use the word "break" in line 5? Does this tell us anything about the city?
Q3. Why do you think the speaker uses the simile "docile as paper" to describe the city?
Q4. If it's not a real place, what do you think the city might represent? Explain your answer.

Memory, loss, individual experiences...

Have a go at comparing the power of memory in this poem and 'Kamikaze'. You could also compare the experience of loss with that in 'Poppies', or the experience of a place with that in 'London'.

Kamikaze

Her father embarked at sunrise
with a flask of water, a samurai sword
in the cockpit, a shaven head
full of powerful incantations
5 and enough fuel for a one-way
journey into history

but half way there, she thought,
recounting it later to her children,
he must have looked far down
10 at the little fishing boats
strung out like bunting
on a green-blue translucent sea

and beneath them, arcing in swathes
like a huge flag waved first one way
15 then the other in a figure of eight,
the dark shoals of fishes
flashing silver as their bellies
swivelled towards the sun

and remembered how he
20 and his brothers waiting on the shore
built cairns of pearl-grey pebbles
to see whose withstood longest
the turbulent inrush of breakers
bringing their father's boat safe

25 *– yes, grandfather's boat –* safe
to the shore, salt-sodden, awash
with cloud-marked mackerel,
black crabs, feathery prawns,
the loose silver of whitebait and once
30 a tuna, the dark prince, muscular, dangerous.

And though he came back
my mother never spoke again
in his presence, nor did she meet his eyes
and the neighbours too, they treated him
35 *as though he no longer existed,*
only we children still chattered and laughed

till gradually we too learned
to be silent, to live as though
he had never returned, that this
40 *was no longer the father we loved.*
And sometimes, she said, he must have wondered
which had been the better way to die.

This creates the sense of a journey, but the title suggests that it will be a journey to his death.

Japan is known as the 'land of the rising sun', so this may be a reference to the location.

This suggests that the pilot was under a kind of spell, which hints at the influence of patriotic propaganda that kamikazes were exposed to. They were told that it was a great honour to die for their country.

Second stanza changes direction — the plane is still flying, but it's going to turn around.

These are the daughter's thoughts and explanations — the pilot has no voice and his real reasons are never heard.

The simile is homely and pretty — a far cry from war. Bunting is associated with celebration, which makes the image ironic — there's no victorious return for the pilot.

Irony — the pilot should have been aiming for big enemy ships, but it's "little fishing boats" that catch his eye.

Beautiful image of nature.

Flags are a symbol of national identity, but here the simile hints at the way that flags can be used to stop or direct something.

The repeated sibilant sounds reflect the smooth movement of the fish in the water.

This hints at the movement of the samurai sword from line 2. It's an ironic reference, because the pilot is turning away from combat.

Focus switches to the pilot's childhood memories.

These are innocent childhood activities, which contrast with the pilot's job in the war.

Enjambment and lack of punctuation in this stanza may hint that the pilot got caught up in his childhood memories.

Repetition of "safe" hints at the pilot's mind-set — he doesn't want his children to go through the pain of losing him.

Interjection of direct speech — it sounds like the pilot's daughter is answering a question from her children.

The colours used — "silver" in this line and "pearl-grey" in line 21 — make nature sound precious.

All the sea creatures are given extra description. The cumulative effect of the list highlights their beauty and significance to the pilot.

The poem's first full stop signals the end of the flight — it should have ended in death, but instead the pilot returns to his family.

Describing the tuna in this way reminds the reader of the dangers of nature.

We hear the daughter's voice in direct speech again. She speaks in a more factual, less descriptive way about her father's subsequent life, which hints at her pain and her empathy with him.

Irony — he survived, but he is still treated as if he's dead.

Hints that the pilot was changed by his experience.

The final, short sentence could be a comment on the destructiveness of patriotism — the pilot's family are so ashamed that they treat him as if he's dead. He may have wished that he'd fulfilled his mission — either way his story ends in a kind of death.

POEM DICTIONARY

kamikaze — one of a group of Japanese WW2 pilots who flew on suicide missions

samurai sword — a traditional Japanese sword

cairns — piles of stones, usually to mark something

breakers — waves that hit the shoreline

Beatrice Garland

Beatrice Garland lives in London and works as a clinician and researcher for the NHS alongside writing poetry. 'Kamikaze' was published in 2013 as part of her first poetry collection, *The Invention of Fireworks*.

You've got to know what the poem's about

1) The poem opens with a kamikaze pilot setting off on his mission. Kamikaze pilots were specially trained Japanese pilots, who were used towards the end of World War Two. They flew their planes on suicide missions into enemy ships — it was seen as a great honour to serve your country in this way.
2) It becomes clear that the pilot turned around and didn't complete his mission — his daughter imagines that this was because on the way he saw the beauty of nature and remembered his innocent childhood.
3) The pilot was shunned when he got home — even his family acted as if he wasn't there.

Learn about the form, structure and language

1) **FORM** — The poem is mostly narrated in the third person using reported speech of the pilot's daughter, but her voice is heard directly in the later stanzas. The absence of the pilot's voice shows that he's been cut off from society, and the use of the third person emphasises the distance between pilot and daughter.
2) **STRUCTURE** — The first five stanzas form one sentence which covers an account of the pilot's flight as the pilot's daughter imagines it. The end of the sentence represents the plane landing, and the final two stanzas deal with the fallout of the pilot's actions.
3) **IRONY** — There are ironic reminders of how the pilot has abandoned his mission. The way he's treated when he returns to his family is ironic because they act as if he's dead, even though he chose not to die.
4) **NATURAL IMAGERY** — Similes, metaphors and detailed descriptions are used to emphasise the beauty and power of nature. The pilot's daughter hints that this beauty was one of the main triggers for his actions.
5) **DIRECT SPEECH** — The addition of direct speech makes the poem seem more personal. Hearing the daughter's voice emphasises the impact of war on a specific family.

Remember the feelings and attitudes in the poem

1) **PATRIOTISM** — The opening stanza is full of suggestions of patriotic pride and duty — the pilot has the chance to fly "into history". The patriotism of his family and neighbours is shown in their reaction to his return — they treat him as if he's dead because he has failed in his duty to his nation.
2) **SHAME** — The reaction of the pilot's wife is one of deep shame — she never speaks to him again.
3) **REGRET** — The pilot's daughter's words in the final stanzas are tinged with a sense of regret and loss. The repetition in lines 9 and 41 of "he must have" also hints at her empathy with the pilot.

Go a step further and give a personal response

Have a go at answering these questions to help you come up with your own ideas about the poem:

Q1. Do you think the main speaker approves of what kamikaze pilots had to do? Why / why not?

Q2. Why do you think we don't hear the pilot's voice in the poem?

Q3. What is the significance of the fish in the poem?

Q4. Do you think the pilot was glad he turned around? Why / why not?

Identity, memory, power of nature...

National identity also features in 'Checking Out Me History'. Try comparing 'Kamikaze' with 'Poppies' if you're writing about memory, and with 'The Prelude' if you're writing about the power of nature.

Checking Out Me History

Dem tell me
Dem tell me
Wha dem want to tell me

Bandage up me eye with me own history
5 Blind me to me own identity

Dem tell me bout 1066 and all dat
dem tell me bout Dick Whittington and he cat
But Toussaint L'Ouverture
no dem never tell me bout dat

10 *Toussaint*
a slave
with vision
lick back
Napoleon
15 *battalion*
and first Black
Republic born
Toussaint de thorn
to de French
20 *Toussaint de beacon*
of de Haitian Revolution

Dem tell me bout de man who discover de balloon
and de cow who jump over de moon
Dem tell me bout de dish ran away with de spoon
25 but dem never tell me bout Nanny de maroon

Nanny
see-far woman
of mountain dream
fire-woman struggle
30 *hopeful stream*
to freedom river

Dem tell me bout Lord Nelson and Waterloo
but dem never tell me bout Shaka de great Zulu
Dem tell me bout Columbus and 1492
35 but what happen to de Caribs and de Arawaks too

Dem tell me bout Florence Nightingale and she lamp
and how Robin Hood used to camp
Dem tell me bout ole King Cole was a merry ole soul
but dem never tell me bout Mary Seacole

40 *From Jamaica*
she travel far
to the Crimean War
she volunteer to go
and even when de British said no
45 *she still brave the Russian snow*
a healing star
among the wounded
a yellow sunrise
to the dying

50 Dem tell me
Dem tell me wha dem want to tell me
But now I checking out me own history
I carving out me identity

Emphasises separateness of the British education system from himself. Repetition of "Dem" and "me" creates a sense of 'them and us'.

Phonetic spelling of Caribbean accent — narrator's voice links to his identity.

Deliberate attempt to hide history. Image of bandage is ironic — bandages should aid healing, but here they've caused blindness.

Repeated phrasing shows that heritage and personal identity are connected.

Metaphor for not allowing him to see his own history.

Dismisses British history — assumes the reader knows it.

Uses pantomime as example — makes British history seem trivial compared to Toussaint.

Succession of short lines slows the pace — suggests he's breaking off from his main point to recall this memory.

Double negative sounds assertive and angry.

Strong rhymes and broken syntax show importance of oral communication.

Images of light and vision contrast with the blindness of his formal education.

Repetition makes it sound like a chant, creating a confident and forceful mood.

Uses nursery rhymes as an example of British history — makes it seem trivial but also links it to the tradition of reciting poems out loud.

Linked to vision — she can see into the future.

The simple rhyme scheme emphasises the silliness of the white history he's been taught. Rhymes build up to last line — highlights what he wasn't taught.

Suggests that she's passionate. Linked to warmth and light.

Connects Nanny to nature and water — she seems like a spiritual person. She's also associated with hope and liberty.

European coloniser compared to native American cultures that resisted slavery — restriction contrasted with freedom. Also a reminder that there's always more than one version of history, but he's only been taught one — that of the colonists.

Makes Florence Nightingale's work sound unimportant and basic. Linked to folklore and nursery rhyme characters in stanza — undermines her.

Figures from British folklore and nursery rhymes contrast with Mary Seacole, an important real-life figure.

Seems more real and relevant than the scenes from white history.

Suggests she's defiant and brave.

Metaphor links her to the wider universe. Images suggest light, hope and warmth.

Repeats phonetic lines from first stanza — reminds us of the narrator's anger.

Emphatic final word — sums up the main theme. He's going to use his own history to create his identity.

POEM DICTIONARY

Toussaint L'Ouverture — a ruler who led the slaves to victory in the Haitian revolution
Nanny de Maroon — leader of the Maroons (runaway slaves), who led Jamaican resistance against the British
Lord Nelson — officer in the Royal Navy who died during the Battle of Trafalgar
Shaka — influential Zulu leader and warrior
Caribs and Arawaks — Caribbean people whose islands were invaded by Europeans
Mary Seacole — Jamaican nurse who helped the sick in the Crimean War

John Agard

John Agard was born in Guyana, a Caribbean country in South America, but he moved to Britain in 1977. His poetry often examines cultures and identities. 'Checking Out Me History' was published in 2007.

You've got to know what the poem's about

1) The narrator is talking about his identity and how it links to his knowledge of history.
2) He was taught about British history but wasn't taught about his Caribbean roots. He lists famous figures from history and questions why he doesn't know about people from other cultures who did great things.
3) He mentions men and women from diverse backgrounds who should be celebrated.
4) At the end, he says he's going to create his own identity based on his heritage.

Learn about the form, structure and language

1) **FORM** — The narrator uses a mixture of stanza forms, suggesting he's breaking the confining language rules he's been taught. The Caribbean history stanzas have shorter lines and more broken syntax than the British history stanzas — this emphasises them and makes them seem more serious. The rhyme schemes are also different — the British stanzas have lots of simple rhymes, making them sound childish.
2) **STRUCTURE** — The poem alternates between historical and fictional figures from Caribbean and British culture, emphasising the differences between them. The British figures are skipped over quickly, with little respect, whereas the Caribbean figures are covered in more detail.
3) **METAPHORS OF VISION AND BLINDNESS** — The narrator says that his education kept his true heritage hidden from him. Images of light are positive because they suggest an awareness of your own identity.
4) **ORAL POETRY FEATURES** — The narrator uses techniques from oral poetry, such as repetition, strong rhythms, chanting and phonetic spellings. This links the poem to the oral tradition of reciting poetry aloud and telling stories, which are used as ways of communicating history. The use of Caribbean phonetic spellings creates a sense of pride in his background, and the use of standard English in lines 46-49 emphasises that the figures from his Caribbean heritage should feature in the teaching of history.

Remember the feelings and attitudes in the poem

1) **ANGER** — The narrator's angry because the education system didn't teach him about his culture. He was unaware of his heritage even though it's an important part of who he is.
2) **ADMIRATION** — He respects the Caribbean figures he describes in the poem. He admires their achievements and wants to tell their stories to show the important role they played in history.
3) **CELEBRATION** — At the end he says he will embrace his own identity in a positive way.

Go a step further and give a personal response

Have a go at answering these questions to help you come up with your own ideas about the poem:

Q1. Why do you think the poet uses both male and female figures from history in the poem?
Q2. What is the effect of the verbs "checking" and "carving" in the final lines of the poem?
Q3. What is the effect of the lack of punctuation in the poem?
Q4. What natural images does the poet use and why are they important?

KEY THEMES

Identity, anger, power of humans...

You could compare the narrator's anger with that of the narrator in 'London'. The formation of identity is a key theme in 'Tissue', where ideas about heritage and challenging authority are also explored.

Practice Questions

Right then, that's the end of the dead bodies, darkrooms and dubious dukes, but now you need to make sure that you've actually learnt something. These questions will check whether the main points of the poems are clear in your head — there are three questions on each poem to get you started.

Ozymandias

1) Who was Ozymandias? Briefly describe his character.
2) What is the effect of having different voices speaking in the poem?
3) How is the power of nature presented in the poem?

London

1) What is the speaker's overall message in the poem?
2) How does the poem convey a sense of hopelessness?
3) What do you think might have been Blake's motivation for writing the poem? Think about the context of the poem.

The Prelude: Stealing the Boat

1) What do you think Wordsworth is saying about man's relationship with nature?
2) How do the narrator's feelings change over the course of the poem?
3) Give an example of personification of the mountain. What is the effect of this?

My Last Duchess

1) What do you think happened to the Duke's last Duchess? Give evidence to support your answer.
2) Describe what we learn about the character of the Duchess. Is this likely to be a fair view of her?
3) What is the effect of the poem being written in rhyming couplets?

The Charge of the Light Brigade

1) Write a brief summary of what happens in each stanza of the poem.
2) How does the narrator feel about the actions of the Light Brigade? How can you tell?
3) Find some examples of repetition in the poem. What is its effect?

Practice Questions

Exposure

1) What do you think the poem's overall message is?
2) Does the tone of the poem change at all? Why do you think this is?
3) What is the effect of the poem's rhyme scheme?

Storm on the Island

1) Briefly explain what the poem is about.
2) What do you think the speaker's overall impression of nature is? Explain your answer.
3) Other than a physical storm, what else might the storm represent? Explain your answer.

Bayonet Charge

1) What is the poem about? What do you think the speaker's message is?
2) What would you say is the overriding emotion in the poem? Explain your answer.
3) Find a metaphor in the poem and explain why it has been used.

Remains

1) What do you think this poem is saying about the effects of conflict on individuals?
2) What is the narrator's tone at the start of the poem? What effect does this have?
3) How is repetition used to show the soldier's guilt?

Poppies

1) What do you think the overall message of the poem is?
2) Describe the speaker's mood in the poem.
3) Why do you think there are so many references to the mother touching things?

Practice Questions

War Photographer

1) What do you think the overall message of the poem is?
2) What do you think the photographer's attitude towards his work is? Explain your answer.
3) What is the rhyme scheme of the poem? What effect does this have?

Tissue

1) Briefly explain what you think the poem is about.
2) How do you think the speaker feels about man-made structures? Explain your answer.
3) Who do you think the "architect" in line 25 might refer to? Explain your answer.

The Emigrée

1) Write a brief summary of each stanza of the poem.
2) What are the main feelings of the speaker in the poem? Do these feelings change at any point?
3) Give an example of personification of the city. What is the effect of this?

Kamikaze

1) Briefly summarise what happens in the poem.
2) How do you think the pilot's daughter feels about her father? Explain your answer.
3) Why do you think the voice switches back to the third person for the final two lines?

Checking Out Me History

1) Give a summary of the speaker's argument in the poem.
2) How does the speaker make the British history he's been taught sound foolish?
3) How is language used to reinforce the speaker's message?

Practice Questions

It's no big secret — the best way to prepare for writing an essay in the exam is... by writing a practice essay. Here are five questions for you to have a crack at — don't forget to plan your answer before you start writing.

Exam-style Questions

1) Compare the way in which the theme of pride is presented in 'My Last Duchess' and one other poem from 'Power and Conflict'.

2) Explore the ways in which the effects of conflict are portrayed in 'The Charge of the Light Brigade' and one other poem from 'Power and Conflict'.

3) Compare the poets' feelings towards a place in 'The Emigrée' and one other poem from 'Power and Conflict'.

4) Explore the ways that ideas about power are presented in 'Tissue' and one other poem from 'Power and Conflict'.

5) 'Those who don't have power are inevitably angry with those who do.'

   Using this quotation as a starting point, write about the theme of anger in 'Checking Out Me History' and one other poem from 'Power and Conflict'.

   Remember to comment on how the poems are written.

Power of Humans

In the exam you'll probably have to compare poems on a given theme — this section covers the likely themes.

1) Humans often use power to benefit themselves rather than other people, and the misuse of power can lead to people being hurt or killed.
2) Human power is ultimately insignificant compared to nature, which is vast and timeless.

Humans can abuse their power...

My Last Duchess (Pages 8-9)

1) The Duke seems obsessed with power — he even controls who sees the portrait of his last duchess.
2) There are hints the Duke had his wife killed — "I gave commands; / Then all smiles stopped" has a sinister tone. Its lack of explanation suggests he doesn't feel he has to account for his actions.
3) The poem's form also reflects his absolute power — although there is a visitor present, we only hear the Duke's voice, and the use of rhyming couplets reflects his rigid control.

Checking Out Me History (Pages 30-31)

1) The speaker in the poem is angry that the people in charge of his education have given him a one-sided view of history — he learnt lots about British history, but nothing about Caribbean heroes.
2) Metaphors of blindness, e.g. "Blind me to me own identity", show how the speaker feels he's been badly treated by those in power.
3) The poem is written with historical misuses of power in mind — it mentions real figures from Caribbean history who revolted against slavery and European colonisation.

...but human power is ultimately temporary

Ozymandias (Pages 2-3)

1) Ozymandias is presented as a ruler who abused his power — he's described as having a "sneer of cold command" and as arrogantly telling other rulers to look at his works and "despair".
2) However, the poem focuses on the temporary nature of the ruler's power. Ozymandias has no power now — there is nothing left of his "works" and even his statue has collapsed.
3) Shelley uses irony to highlight the contrast between Ozymandias's belief in his own power and the reality that all his achievements are insignificant compared to the "boundless" desert.

Tissue (Pages 24-25)

1) Paper is used to symbolise human power — receipts can "fly our lives like paper kites", but they're fragile and easily destroyed, hinting at its impermanence. Paper maps show "borderlines" and other man-made features, but the sun "shines through" them, alluding to nature's enduring power.
2) In the eighth stanza, the speaker talks about letting "daylight break / through capitals and monoliths". This is an image of natural power being greater than human power — "capitals and monoliths" represent human governments and buildings, but they are temporary compared to nature.

Think about the role of human power in other poems...

The speaker in 'London' is frustrated about the misuse of human power — he feels that it's used to control rather than to help people. In 'Storm on the Island', human power is insignificant compared to nature.

Power of Nature

Ahh, nature — I'm thinking of a sunny spring morning filled with daffodils and ducklings. Sadly not...

1) Nature is a powerful force that can cause suffering and destruction. It's often personified in poetry to describe its effect in human terms.
2) Nature has the power to change humans and affect their decisions.

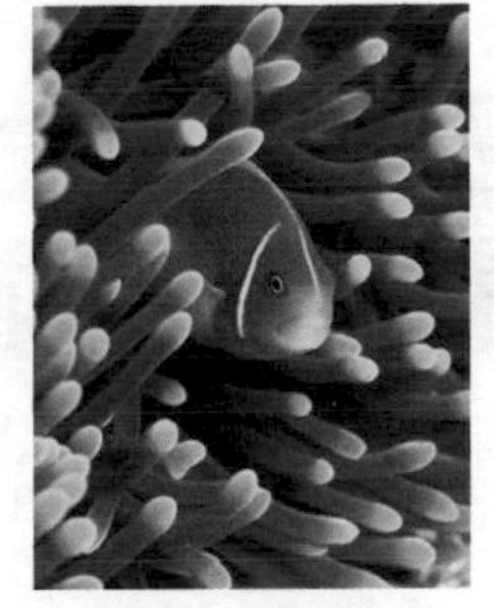

Sam decided to present nature as an anemone instead.

Nature is presented as an enemy

Exposure (Pages 12-13)

1) Nature is personified as the deadly enemy of the soldiers in the trenches — it has "merciless iced east winds that knive" them, and snowflakes that "come feeling" for their faces with "fingering stealth". The men expect to die not from German gunfire, but from exposure to the elements.
2) There's no progression in the poem, which mirrors the relentlessness of nature. The repeated stanza ending, "But nothing happens", echoes the monotonous snow and rain that falls on the men.

Storm on the Island (Pages 14-15)

1) There are two aspects of nature described in the poem, and both have a negative effect on the islanders.
2) The island is inhospitable because nothing can grow there — the earth is "wizened" and there are no trees or "stacks / Or stooks".
3) However, it's the extremes of nature that the islanders fear — war imagery is used to suggest that nature is attacking the island — it's "bombarded by the empty air" and the wind "strafes" it.

Nature can have a powerful effect on humans

The Prelude: Stealing the Boat (Pages 6-7)

1) The almost magical beauty of nature is present in the poem, with the "circles glittering" on the lake and the "sparkling light". The narrator initially seems to be inspired and relaxed by nature.
2) However, when a mountain appears, it is personified as a terrifying, monstrous being — it "Upreared its head" and the narrator thinks that it "Strode after" him. It seems to be this that makes him return the boat he stole, suggesting that nature is able to influence our behaviour.
3) The poem ends with the phrase "a trouble to my dreams." This acts as a reminder of how nature is not just beautiful and gentle — the narrator has been unsettled and changed by the experience, and the "pleasant images" of nature in his mind have been replaced with troubling ones.

Kamikaze (Pages 28-29)

1) Nature is presented as one of the reasons why the pilot turned back — his daughter thought that seeing the beauty of the scene below him compelled him to abandon his mission.
2) The danger of nature is also alluded to, with the "turbulent inrush" of waves and the "muscular, dangerous" tuna. This suggests that humans are at the mercy of nature — the "turbulent" waves could crush a boat, or a fisherman could be dragged overboard by a tuna.

Some poems compare natural power with human power...

'Ozymandias' and 'Tissue' both present nature as being stronger than humans. In 'Tissue', sunlight breaks through man-made structures, and in 'Ozymandias', Shelley shows nature outlasting the ruler's power.

Effects of Conflict

Death, death and more death — that's the gist of it, but thankfully the poets are a bit more creative than that.

1) Conflict causes injury (both physical and psychological) and death.
2) Even people not directly involved in the fighting can be affected by conflict.

Conflict affects the people who fight...

The Charge of the Light Brigade (Pages 10-11)

1) Death or serious injury is the ultimate result of the battle for many of the soldiers. The repetition of phrases like "valley of Death" and "mouth of Hell" creates an ominous mood and confirms there is no escaping their fate.
2) The speaker focuses on the extensive loss of life in the charge — each stanza ends with a reference to the "six hundred" to remind the reader of the huge human cost involved.
3) The poem also shows how war can inspire great bravery and sacrifice. The soldiers do their duty even though they believe they are probably going to die in the process.

Remains (Pages 18-19)

1) The soldier dehumanises the looter and presents the killing as a normal part of his job, as shown by the poem's anecdotal tone and opening phrase, "On another occasion". Colloquial verbs like "tosses" and "carted off" describe how the soldiers casually dispose of the body. This suggests that conflict can devalue human life and make violence seem normal.
2) However, memories of conflict have a deep psychological impact on the soldier (see p.41).
3) The final stanza of the poem is made up of only two lines rather than the normal four — the disruption of the poem's form mirrors the soldier's breakdown.

...and those who don't

Poppies (Pages 20-21)

1) 'Poppies' focuses on the pain and distress experienced by a mother whose son has joined the army.
2) Even before he goes, the mother feels detached from her son — the "gelled / blackthorns" of his hair stop her running her fingers through it. This emotional distance foreshadows their physical separation.
3) After the son leaves, the mother is anxious and restless. Her fear for his safety is revealed in physical symptoms — she describes her stomach as "busy / making tucks, darts, pleats".

War Photographer (Pages 22-23)

1) In the war zone, the photographer is able to keep a steady hand, but as he develops the photos, his hands "tremble", suggesting that he is deeply affected by the "hundred agonies" he has seen.
2) His view of home is also affected by his experience of war — the "ordinary pain" of England contrasts starkly with that of "running children in a nightmare heat" in the war zone.
3) The final stanza considers the reactions to conflict of people not involved in it. The emphatic "they do not care" implies that people have become so desensitised to suffering that it no longer affects them.

These poems also consider the effects of conflict...

'Kamikaze' shows the effects of conflict on the pilot and his family. 'The Emigrée' contains hints that conflict forced the speaker to leave the city. 'Exposure' and 'Bayonet Charge' both show ideals being lost in war.

Reality of Conflict

The reality of conflict can be pretty painful — I should know, I grew up with two brothers...

1) Poems set in the heat of the battle create vivid pictures of the sights, sounds and emotions.
2) Poems set after the battle are more detached from the reality.

The horror of war can be described as it happens...

Exposure (Pages 12-13)

1) Bleak imagery is used to convey the men's pain — for example, the description of the frost as "puckering foreheads crisp" compels the reader to imagine their flesh freezing. Comparing the noise of the wind to the "twitching agonies of men" creates a vivid picture of wounded soldiers.
2) The reality of war leaves no room for patriotism or heroism — the men "cringe in holes" like frightened animals. Rhetorical questions ("What are we doing here?") emphasise the pointlessness of their suffering.
3) The hopeless tone of the poem suggests that the men believe they have little chance of surviving. They seem to have accepted that they will never see their families or homes again.

Bayonet Charge (Pages 16-17)

1) The soldier is presented as a confused and helpless victim — he is "running" in a state of bewilderment, and verbs like "Stumbling" suggest he has no control of his situation or actions.
2) His discomfort is clear from his "raw-seamed hot khaki" and the way he "lugged" his rifle. Violent imagery, such as the "Bullets smacking the belly out of the air", hint that he may be in pain.
3) Physical descriptions of the battle create a sense of noise and confusion. The "blue crackling air" gives the impression that the soldier is completely surrounded by danger.
4) His patriotism and principles are "Dropped like luxuries" — they are no use to him in the heat of battle.

...or after the event

The Charge of the Light Brigade (Pages 10-11)

1) The poem creates a noisy and frightening picture of the battle using onomatopoeia ("thunder'd"), violent verbs ("Flash'd") and a relentless, galloping rhythm. This emphasises the men's bravery and heroism.
2) However, there's a distance between the speaker and the battlefield — the battle is recounted like a story, and the chronological structure helps impose order on the events.

Remains (Pages 18-19)

1) War forces people to make morally complicated decisions on the spur of the moment. The soldier is left with a disturbing feeling of responsibility, as shown by the phrase "his bloody life in my bloody hands."
2) Graphic images present the reader with a vivid picture of the horror of war — the speaker describes seeing "broad daylight" through the bullet holes in the looter, which is a grotesque, disturbing image.
3) The soldier is unable to remain detached from the reality of what he's done — his sleep is interrupted by repeated images of the man being "torn apart" and he is haunted by his memories.

You could also write about 'War Photographer'...

The photographer is not actively involved in conflict, but he sees the reality of it on a daily basis. Emotive imagery like the "running children in a nightmare heat" is used to create a picture of the horrors of war.

Loss and Absence

Two more cheery, uplifting themes here, but hey, it could be worse — at least this isn't chemistry...

1) People experience loss when they're separated from someone or something they love.
2) An absence of hope can lead to negativity and despair.

Conflict can cause loss of people or places

Poppies (Pages 20-21)

1) The mother feels like she's lost her son when he leaves to join the army. She acts almost as if he has died — she leans against the "war memorial" and mentions "Armistice Sunday".
2) The loss she experiences is emphasised by references to textures and the senses. She traces "the inscriptions" on the war memorial and listens for her son's voice "on the wind" — this hints at her desperate desire to find some kind of connection with him, to compensate for their separation.

The Emigrée (Pages 26-27)

1) The speaker is nostalgic for a place that she left as a child — the opening phrase "There once was a country..." frames the poem with the sense of loss she feels for the place. This loss is heightened by the fact that the speaker retains an "impression of sunlight" — a positive, idealised view of the city.
2) There are suggestions that conflict is responsible for the speaker's loss — the city "may be at war", and the speaker describes herself as an "Emigrée" in the title, hinting that she was forced to leave.

Kamikaze (Pages 28-29)

1) Although the pilot chose to avoid dying in the war, his family still lose him — their shame causes them to treat him "as though he no longer existed".
2) The daughter's statement that he "was no longer the father we loved" hints at the pain that this emotional loss caused both the pilot and his family.

People without power often feel hopeless

London (Pages 4-5)

1) There's an absence of anything positive in the poem — the speaker refers to the absence of freedom ("the chartered Thames"), innocence ("Blasts the new-born infant's tear") and morality ("harlot's curse").
2) There's also an absence of hope, with no sense that anyone can do anything to improve the situation. The final image of the plagued "marriage hearse" implies the cycle of suffering will continue.

Exposure (Pages 12-13)

1) The men in the trenches have no hope of things improving. The dejected line, "We only know war lasts, rain soaks and clouds sag stormy" emphasises that their lives are miserable and filled with suffering.
2) Even thinking about home doesn't provide any hope for the men — they understand that they are "dying" and know that at home "the doors are closed" to them.

Loss of life is a common theme in this cluster...

The speaker in 'The Charge of the Light Brigade' is keen to emphasise the loss of life, repeating "the six hundred". Conversely, the Duke in 'My Last Duchess' doesn't seem to feel loss, despite his wife's death.

Memory

They say an elephant never forgets, but it turns out soldiers, photographers, mothers and pilots don't either...

1) Memories can be powerful, particularly memories of negative or difficult experiences.
2) Memories often contain specific, personal details which give them a unique power.

Memories can have a haunting effect

Remains (Pages 18-19)

1) The speaker is haunted by the memory of killing the looter. Going home doesn't help him, his sleep is disturbed and he can't "flush" out the memory with "drink" or "drugs".
2) The monosyllabic, punchy line openings of "Sleep" and "Dream" imitate the loud, violent sounds of bullet shots, and reflect the way that he is jolted awake at night by memories of the killing.
3) The metaphor of a soldier "dug in behind enemy lines" emphasises how the memory is stuck in his mind, and hints at the danger of the memory — it has the potential to destroy him.

Ted (top) had happier memories of winning the squadron's human pyramid tournament.

War Photographer (Pages 22-23)

1) The photographer's memories are triggered by the development of a photo in his darkroom.
2) Senses are used to describe his memories — he remembers hearing "the cries / of this man's wife" and seeing the "blood stained" in the dust. This makes them seem personal and vivid in his mind.
3) The way that his hands "tremble" suggests that remembering the scenes is difficult — the memories of conflicts seem to affect him more deeply than the original events did.

Memories can be described vividly

The Emigrée (Pages 26-27)

1) The speaker vividly remembers the city she left as a child. She describes her view of it as a "bright, filled paperweight", showing how her memories are positive, colourful and solid. Different senses increase the vividness — her "child's vocabulary" "tastes of sunlight" and she combs the personified city's "hair".
2) However, there's a suggestion that the speaker's memories are unreliable — the perfect place she remembers might be "at war" or "sick with tyrants".

Kamikaze (Pages 28-29)

1) The pilot's daughter imagines that the pilot's idyllic childhood memories contributed to him turning round.
2) The vivid, beautiful descriptions of sea creatures hint at the power of the pilot's childhood memories. Metaphors like the "loose silver of whitebait" create a powerful, sensual picture.
3) In contrast, the daughter's memories of life after her father's return are presented in a matter-of-fact way — her straightforward language ("my mother never spoke again") shows how painful the situation was.

Other poems also feature powerful memories...

The speaker in 'The Prelude' is deeply troubled by his memories of the mountain. The mother in 'Poppies' clings to her memories of her son, both as a small boy and when he leaves to join the army.

Negative Emotions

These poems have so much negativity that we need two pages. Good job every other theme is so positive...

The poems in the cluster express a range of negative emotions, for example:

1) Anger is a strong emotion that often stems from a hurtful experience or a sense of mistreatment.
2) Guilt is often associated with conflict, either because of actions committed in war, or because of being able to escape a war that other people cannot.
3) Fear is often experienced in response to uncontrollable forces, such as nature or war.
4) Pride is linked to power, and it often leads to a misuse of that power.

Anger can be directed at society

London (Pages 4-5)

1) The narrator is angry about the society he sees as he wanders the streets of London.
2) He uses rhetorical devices to get the reader to share his anger. For example, he repeats "marks" and "every" and uses emotive imagery, such as "every infant's cry of fear".
3) The images of the "black'ning church" and "blood down palace walls" show his anger at institutions like the Church and the government / monarchy for not improving things.

Checking Out Me History (Pages 30-31)

1) The speaker is angry at British society for giving him an education that ignored his Caribbean heritage.
2) He repeats the phrase "Dem tell me" to set himself ("me") in clear opposition to society ("Dem"). He avoids using standard British grammar to distance himself from the society he's criticising.
3) His anger leads him to juxtapose British pantomime and nursery rhyme characters, e.g. "Dick Whittington and he cat", with Caribbean heroes, e.g. "Toussaint L'Ouverture". These comparisons are deliberately ridiculous, emphasising his frustration with "Dem" in a humorous way.

War can leave people feeling guilty

Remains (Pages 18-19)

1) The soldier's guilt seems to stem from his doubt as to whether or not the looter was armed. The repetition of "probably armed, possibly not" shows that he's replaying the action in his mind and trying to work out if his actions were justified.
2) The guilt eats away at the soldier — he says the dead man is "here in my head when I close my eyes". The potential reference to Lady Macbeth in the final line hints that guilt is driving the soldier mad.
3) The shift of voice from first person plural ("we") to first person singular ("I") shows that the soldier feels personally responsible for the death. This is confirmed in the final line, where emphasis falls on "my".

War Photographer (Pages 22-23)

1) There's a sense that the photographer feels guilty about the ease of life in England. The phrase, "ordinary pain which simple weather can dispel", shows how different life in England is from life in a war zone.
2) He refers to taking the picture as doing "what someone must". There's an element of guilt to his words — he knows that taking photographs may seem insensitive, but he feels a duty to record the moment and make sure that the world's attention is drawn to this suffering.

Negative Emotions

People fear situations they cannot understand or control

The Prelude: Stealing the Boat (Pages 6-7)

1) The narrator's mood changes from carefree confidence to deep fear after encountering the mountain. This fear has a lasting effect, with the experience troubling his thoughts and dreams "for many days".
2) The mountain's solid "stature" and "measured motion" is contrasted with the speaker's "trembling"— the personified mountain is calm and in control, whereas the speaker is frantically trying to escape.

Storm on the Island (Pages 14-15)

1) There is also a progression from security to fear in 'Storm on the Island'. The confident opening of "We are prepared" has changed to a confession of "fear" by the end of the poem.
2) The fear is amplified because nature is an invisible, abstract force — the speaker calls the storm "a huge nothing". This highlights the fact that the islanders can do nothing to combat it.
3) The image of the "tame cat / Turned savage" shows how even familiar things become scary in the storm.

Bayonet Charge (Pages 16-17)

1) Beginning the poem *in medias res* (in the middle of things) immediately alerts the reader to the soldier's fear. The opening description, "Suddenly he awoke and was running", hints that the soldier is not really in control of his body — it's like he's trapped in a nightmare.
2) The soldier's terror is shown by repeated references to his sweat — a bodily fluid associated with fear. Even his rifle is "numb", suggesting that he's almost paralysed with fear.
3) The final metaphor of "His terror's touchy dynamite" suggests his fear has overwhelmed him.

Too much pride can lead to arrogance

Ozymandias (Pages 2-3)

1) The words on the pedestal of the statue show that Ozymandias was a proud, arrogant ruler. He calls himself the "king of kings" and commands other rulers to "Look" at his works and "despair".
2) The reference to his "sneer of cold command" suggests that he thought everyone else was inferior to him, and that he treated his subjects badly.

My Last Duchess (Pages 8-9)

1) The Duke is proud of his name, art collection and reputation. What he viewed as the flirtatious behaviour of his last Duchess hurt his pride — she didn't appreciate his "gift of a nine-hundred-years-old name".
2) The poem hints that this all led to the Duchess's death — the Duke arrogantly boasts that he was too proud even to criticise her behaviour ("I choose / Never to stoop"). Instead he had her killed.
3) Several of the Duke's comments to his visitor also display his arrogance, e.g. "Will't please you sit and look at her?" is almost a command — the visitor has no choice but to sit and admire the portrait.

Hopelessness is another negative emotion to think about...

There are several poems where situations seem hopeless, including 'London' and 'Exposure' (see p.4
Think about how poets present hopeless scenes, and the effect hopelessness has on the people invo

Identity

I don't know what this 'ity' is — it's usually cars, walls or my bank balance that I dent...

1) Belonging to a family is an important part of human identity.
2) National identity and patriotism can have powerful effects, particularly in war.

Family identity is precious

Poppies (Pages 20-21)

1) The boy's identity as a son is clearly established in the poem — his mother smooths down his collar and mentions that they used to "play at / being Eskimos" when he was younger.
2) However, the son has a new identity as a soldier — his "blazer" is a visual reminder of this. The mother moving from his bedroom to the "war memorial" reflects this change — the bedroom is a symbol of family identity, but the war memorial symbolises his new identity as a soldier.
3) The mother still clings to his identity as her son and the poem ends with her trying to hear his "playground voice" — he's still her child and she longs for him to return to her.

Tissue (Pages 24-25)

1) The opening three stanzas explore the importance of family history and heritage — there's a reference to recording family histories in "the back of the Koran".
2) These pages are treasured — they are "smoothed and stroked", almost as if they were living things. The repetition of this phrase later in the poem, in reference to the "grand design" of a human body, shows how important family history and heritage is in forming an individual's identity.

Buster wished his owner would stroke him rather than pages in a book.

National identity has a powerful influence on people

Kamikaze (Pages 28-29)

1) National identity often becomes more important in times of war. During World War Two, many Japanese people saw it as a great honour to be a kamikaze and die for their country. The "incantations" that fill the pilot's head may refer to the patriotic propaganda used by the government to promote national identity.
2) However, the pilot's decision to turn around was unpatriotic — he failed in his duty to his country.
3) The end of the poem explores the tension between family identity and national identity. For the pilot, family identity was more important, but his family's patriotism was so strong that they treated him as if he was dead, meaning that he lost his identity as a husband and a father.

Checking Out Me History (Pages 30-31)

1) The speaker feels that his personal identity has been shaped too much by British national identity.
2) He believes that learning about key figures in Caribbean history will help develop his true identity.
3) The poem ends with the speaker's assertion that he is "carving out me identity". The forceful statement shows he intends to continue learning — "carving" hints at a difficult process with a permanent result.

National identity is also important to Tennyson's speaker...

The speaker in 'The Charge of the Light Brigade' believes that the men should be honoured as national heroes. He praises them for their display of bravery and for following their orders without question.

Individual Experiences

No friends, no lovers, no-one to share experiences with — yep, that sounds about right for this lot...

1) Conflicts can involve thousands of people, but everyone involved has their own experience of it.
2) Focusing on individual experiences allows the poet to present a place, action or event from a specific, unique point of view.

Conflict can leave individuals feeling isolated

Bayonet Charge (Pages 16-17)

1) There are no other soldiers present in the poem — the soldier seems isolated and alone.
2) The only other living thing is a "yellow hare" that gruesomely crawls "in a threshing circle". Focusing on a single animal mirrors the soldier's isolation and emphasises how far he is from any help or comfort.
3) The soldier feels he's ultimately insignificant in the "cold clockwork of the stars and the nations". Although he understands that he's part of a wider picture, he feels completely isolated from it.

War Photographer (Pages 22-23)

1) The photographer is described as being "finally alone" — this could suggest that he needs space and quiet to reflect on his experiences, but also hints at his guilt about being able to escape the "suffering".
2) His isolation in the war zone is highlighted by the fact that it's a "stranger's features" he photographs, and that he seeks approval "without words" from the man's wife. Although he records people's suffering, he doesn't share in it — this distances him from them.
3) The emphatic closing remark of "they do not care" emphasises how different he feels from everyone else — the ambiguity surrounding who "they" are hints that he feels isolated from the rest of the world.

Individuals have unique experiences of places

London (Pages 4-5)

1) The poem opens with "I" and takes the form of a dramatic monologue describing a walk through London.
2) The speaker seems to be removed from the suffering he sees, allowing him to observe and comment on the bigger picture. This means that he can recognise the "mind-forged manacles" that trap people, and he can criticise institutions like the monarchy and the church for their corruption and lack of action.
3) The speaker's description of the city is entirely negative, which makes the reader question whether he's biased. Even in the joyful event of a wedding he can only picture a funeral ("the marriage hearse").

The Prelude: Stealing the Boat (Pages 6-7)

1) The narrator is alone in his "act of stealth" as he takes the boat and sets out across the lake. When the mountain frightens him, he describes it in personal terms, claiming that the mountain "Strode after me". This personification suggests that he feels nature is reacting to him as an individual.
2) He describes the effect the event has on him as "solitude / Or blank desertion", emphasising how the event has left him isolated and alone. His view of nature has been changed and he's left feeling insignificant compared with the "huge and mighty forms" of nature.

Other poems also focus on individual experiences...

The speaker in 'The Emigrée' seems alone in her views of her old city and appears isolated in the new city, where other people threaten her. 'Remains' looks at one soldier struggling to deal with his experiences.

Practice Questions

There are some exam-style questions just around the corner, but first here are some questions that you don't need to write a full essay to answer. One or two short paragraphs should be enough.

Power of Humans

1) How is the Duke's power and control emphasised in 'My Last Duchess'?
2) Describe two examples of human misuse of power from 'Checking Out Me History'.
3) How does Dharker present human power as temporary in 'Tissue'?

Power of Nature

1) Do you think nature is more powerful in 'Exposure' or 'Storm on the Island'? Explain your answer.
2) In the extract from 'The Prelude', how does the speaker's understanding of nature's power change?
3) How is the power of nature significant in 'Kamikaze'?

Effects of Conflict

1) How does Tennyson create a sense of the men's heroism in 'The Charge of the Light Brigade'?
2) Do you think that the speaker in 'Remains' regrets killing the looter? Why / Why not?
3) In 'Poppies', how does the mother's separation from her son affect her actions?

Reality of Conflict

1) How does the tone of 'Exposure' help to convey the reality of war?
2) How is the horror of war depicted in 'Bayonet Charge'?
3) In 'The Charge of the Light Brigade', how does the poet create a vivid picture of the battlefield?

Loss and Absence

1) How is the speaker's sense of loss presented in 'The Emigrée'?
2) What does the pilot in 'Kamikaze' lose? How is this presented?
3) In 'London', how does the image of the "marriage hearse" emphasise the absence of hope?

Practice Questions

Memory

1) Who do you think is more affected by memories of war, the photographer in 'War Photographer' or the soldier in 'Remains'? Explain your answer.

2) How is the speaker in 'The Emigrée' influenced by her memories of her city?

3) In 'Kamikaze', how is memory presented as a powerful force on a) the pilot and b) his daughter?

Negative Emotions

1) How does Blake present the speaker's anger in 'London'?

2) How does the speaker in 'Checking Out Me History' use humour to support his anger?

3) In 'War Photographer', why does the photographer feel guilty? How does his guilt affect him?

4) How is the feeling of fear developed in a similar way in 'The Prelude' and in 'Storm on the Island'?

5) In 'Bayonet Charge', how does Hughes create a vivid picture of the soldier's fear?

6) Why do you think Shelley chose to emphasise the arrogance of the ruler in 'Ozymandias'?

Identity

1) In 'Poppies', how is the mother affected by her son's new identity?

2) How does the speaker in 'Tissue' present family history as being important?

3) How are personal and national identity connected for the speaker in 'Checking Out Me History'?

Individual Experiences

1) How does the poet create the sense that the photographer in 'War Photographer' is isolated?

2) In 'London', what evidence is there that the speaker's experience of the city might be biased?

3) In the extract from 'The Prelude', why is it significant that the speaker is alone?

Practice Questions

In the exam you'll have to compare two poems which share a common theme, so no prizes for guessing what these questions are going to ask you to do. Don't try and do them all in one go — choose one, jot down a plan and have a crack at writing an answer. Then come back tomorrow and try another one.

Exam-style Questions

1) Man is often portrayed as being in conflict with nature. Explore the ways in which nature is portrayed as the enemy of man in 'Exposure' and one other poem from 'Power and Conflict'.

2) Compare the way in which the reality of war is presented in 'Bayonet Charge' and one other poem from 'Power and Conflict'.

3) Compare the way that poets present loss in 'Poppies' and one other poem from 'Power and Conflict'.

4) Compare the way that negative feelings are presented in 'London' and in one other poem from 'Power and Conflict'.

5) "There is no type of identity that is more important than family identity."

   Using this quotation as a starting point, write about the theme of identity in 'Kamikaze' and one other poem from 'Power and Conflict'.

   Remember to comment on how the poems are written.

Forms of Poetry

Form is about the rules poets follow when writing poetry. And like all good rules, they're there to be broken...

1) Form can be rigid and regular or loose and irregular.
2) Poets choose a form to create different moods and effects.

Some poems have a strict, regular form...

Exposure (Pages 12-13)

1) The poem has a rigid form, with eight similar stanzas that each have four long lines and a half-line at the end. There's also a regular ABBAC rhyme scheme.
2) This form reflects the monotonous existence of the soldiers in the trenches. There is no hope of change for the men, and the half-lines at the end of each stanza reinforce this — the gaps they leave emphasise the lack of action or hope.

War Photographer (Pages 22-23)

1) The poem consists of four six-line stanzas, each with lines of similar length and a regular ABBCDD rhyme scheme. The regularity of the poem reflects the photographer's work — the poem is made up of "ordered rows", just like the "spools" he lays out in his darkroom.
2) This regular form echoes the careful, methodical process that the photographer goes through.
3) It also highlights a similarity between the work of the photographer and that of the poet — just as the photographs put the suffering of war into "black and white", the poem presents the dangerous and unpredictable work of the war photographer in an ordered and comprehensible way.

...whereas others have a less rigid form

The Charge of the Light Brigade (Pages 10-11)

1) Tennyson uses an irregular form to reflect the chaos of war — it is made up of six unique stanzas, each with between six and twelve lines and a different rhyme scheme.
2) Although there's no regular rhyme scheme, lots of rhyme is used to drive the poem forwards like the galloping cavalry. Rhyming triplets like "reply", "why" and "die" create momentum that's then broken by an unrhymed line ("Death"). This mirrors the stumbling of the horses as they're shot at.

Checking Out Me History (Pages 30-31)

1) The poem uses different stanza forms to separate the humorous attacks on British historical and cultural figures from the serious details about heroic Caribbean figures.
2) The British stanzas are all quatrains — this regular form mirrors the speaker's restrictive education, especially when contrasted with the free verse and song-like chants used in the Caribbean stanzas.
3) The Caribbean stanzas are presented in italics with short, sometimes one-word lines. These short lines slow the pace of the poem, forcing you to pay attention to the stories described.

Other poems use specific forms...

'Ozymandias' is a sonnet, although it doesn't use a traditional sonnet rhyme scheme. 'My Last Duchess' is a dramatic monologue, where a single speaker (the Duke) addresses an implied audience (the visitor).

Poetic Devices

If your teacher's told you to write about it, and it's got a fancy name, there's a good chance it's a poetic device.

1) Poets use all kinds of devices to liven up their writing. These pages pick out a few of the important ones, but there are lots more you could write about.
2) You need to be able to identify different techniques used in the poems and make comparisons between them.
3) It's really important that you don't just say what the technique is, but comment on the effect that it has on the poem.

Punctuation affects how a poem flows

Tissue (Pages 24-25)

1) Lots of lines and stanzas defy restrictions and flow into the next — this enjambment reflects the freedom that the speaker longs for.
2) The fifth stanza presents a contrast between the freedom of nature and the restrictiveness of human constructs like "borderlines". This contrast is emphasised by the use of enjambment ("The sun shines through / their borderlines") and caesura ("Maps too.")

The Emigrée (Pages 26-27)

1) Enjambment in the first two stanzas of 'The Emigrée' mirrors the freedom the speaker had in the city she left. Phrases like "the graceful slopes / glow" suggest that she was free and life was easy there.
2) This enjambment suggests that the speaker is absorbed in her memories and gets carried away describing them. She enjoys remembering and speaking about the city.
3) However, in the final stanza, each line is end-stopped. This reflects how the speaker sees her new city as a "city of walls". There's a sense that the speaker feels restricted.

Repetition reinforces a point

The Charge of the Light Brigade (Pages 10-11)

1) There are repeated references to the "six hundred" men who made up the Light Brigade — repetition of the number emphasises the human cost of the battle.
2) Tennyson also uses repetition to develop a vivid picture of the battlefield. The repetition of phrases such as "valley of Death" and "mouth of Hell" creates a horrific, frightening scene.
3) In the third and fifth stanzas, repetition of "Cannon to right of them, / Cannon to left of them", emphasises how the Light Brigade are completely surrounded by Russian gunfire.

Remains (Pages 18-19)

1) The speaker in 'Remains' uses repetition early on in the poem to create the sense that the looter's death was a collective act. In the second stanza, "all", "three" and "somebody else" are repeated to highlight that other people were involved. However, this repetition makes the point feel almost over-emphasised — it hints that the speaker may be trying to shift responsibility from himself.
2) The phrase "probably armed, possibly not" from the first stanza is repeated in the sixth stanza. This highlights the way that the speaker keeps replaying the looter's death in his mind.

Poetic Devices

Irony can highlight the gap between expectations and reality

Ozymandias (Pages 2-3)

"Some would say it's ironic that although I have no power left, you still have to learn about me..."

1) 'Ozymandias' focuses on the irony that the king's achievements are ultimately worthless — all that's left of his kingdom is a ruined statue.
2) The inscription on the statue's base is ironic with hindsight — the king warned other rulers to "despair" when they saw his "works", but none of his creations are left now.
3) The irony also challenges the reader to consider their own view of human achievement — many people are similarly blind in their quest for power.

Kamikaze (Pages 28-29)

1) The pilot's reception when he returns home is ironic. He chose not to die when he abandoned his mission, but his family's shame led them to treat him as if he was dead anyway.
2) There are ironic reminders of the pilot's failure to complete his mission — for example he sees "boats / strung out like bunting", but there will be no celebrations of the pilot's heroism.
3) The irony is ultimately tragic — the poem's closing lines are poignant as they question whether it would have been "better" for the pilot if he had completed his suicide mission.

Poets appeal to the senses to create a vivid picture

London (Pages 4-5)

1) The poem is based around the scenes the speaker sees as he walks around the streets of London — the images of "marks of woe" on "every face", the "black'ning church" and the "blood" that runs down "palace walls" combine to create a picture of pain, corruption and death.
2) Sounds are also important — the combination of the "infant's cry of fear", the "chimney-sweeper's cry" and the "youthful harlot's curse" create a noisy, unpleasant impression of the city.

Poppies (Pages 20-21)

1) The mother's memories of her son are very physical (e.g. "graze my nose" and "playground voice").
2) Before he goes she touches his collar and removes "cat hairs" from his shirt, but restrains from stroking his hair — their physical connection has lessened as he's grown up, and now he physically leaves her.
3) In the final stanza, the mother leans against the war memorial and "traced / the inscriptions" on it — she needs to physically touch something to feel connected to her son.

The Emigrée (Pages 26-27)

1) The speaker's positive associations with the past and the city are emphasised by the use of sight and taste.
2) Imagery of light ("white streets" and "slopes / glow") creates an almost heavenly picture of the city.
3) The speaker says her "child's vocabulary" "tastes of sunlight" — the recollection of an element of her childhood in the city generates a strong, physical sensation of pleasure.

You could also think about the use of contrasts...

Lots of the poems use contrasts for emphasis, e.g. oxymorons in 'London' show how even innocent things have been corrupted, and in 'Bayonet Charge', the reality of war contrasts starkly with patriotic ideals.

Use of Sound

Poems are often intended to be read aloud, so the sounds words make are particularly important.

1) Onomatopoeia is an effective way of adding dramatic sounds to a poem.
2) Poets repeat similar sounds to create a particular mood or effect, e.g. sibilant sounds create a hissing noise which can be threatening or unsettling.

Onomatopoeia can mimic the noise of a battlefield

The Charge of the Light Brigade (Pages 10-11)

1) Onomatopoeic verbs like "thunder'd" and "Shatter'd" imitate the chaotic, deafening noise of battle.
2) By replicating the powerful, threatening noise of the battlefield, Tennyson shows how frightening it must have been, and emphasises the heroism of the Light Brigade.

Bayonet Charge (Pages 16-17)

1) In the opening stanza, the onomatopoeic verb "smacking" creates a loud and jarring effect with its harsh 'c' sound. It acts as a violent reminder of the dangers the soldier faces.
2) The "crackling air" in the final stanza sounds dangerous and emphasises the fact that the soldier is completely surrounded by gunfire — nowhere is safe.

Repeated sounds create different effects

The Prelude: Stealing the Boat (Pages 6-7)

1) The repetition of sibilant sounds in lines 24-29 (e.g. "struck", "still", "stars") emphasises the sinister way that the mountain seems to glide after the narrator. This creates a threatening mood that reflects his fear.
2) Repetition of gentle 'l' sounds (e.g. "Small", "still", "melted all") creates consonance in lines 8-11. This produces a flowing effect, which reflects the gentle movement of the boat across the lake.

Exposure (Pages 12-13)

1) Assonance is used to emphasise the men's painful experience — long 'oh' sounds are repeated in the third stanza ("grow", "only know", "soaks") and sixth stanza ("Slowly our ghosts drag home"). The drawn out sounds reflect the men's exhaustion and the long, monotonous days in the trenches.
2) Owen uses sibilance to recreate the noise of the battlefield — the line "Sudden successive flights of bullets streak the silence" imitates the sound of bullets whistling through the air.

Storm on the Island (Pages 14-15)

1) Phrases such as "spray hits" and "spits" contain sibilant, assonant 'i' and plosive sounds. These combine to imitate the fitful spitting sound of sea spray, which contributes to the "savage" description of the sea.
2) The wind is also described using sibilant sounds — it "dives / And strafes invisibly. Space is a salvo." — this imitates the wind whistling across the island. Plosive sounds, e.g. "Space" and "bombarded", create a sense of sudden gusts of wind, which add to the feelings of uncertainty and fear.

Alliteration is another poetic use of sound...

Dharker uses alliteration ("rivers... roads, / railtracks") in 'Tissue' to hint at freedom from human constraints. In 'Poppies', the alliterative "hoping to hear" emphasises the mother's deep longing for her son's safe return.

Imagery

Imagery is when a poet uses language to create a picture — it includes similes, metaphors and personification.

1) Personification can make things seem more real or lifelike.
2) Similes and metaphors create powerful descriptions.

Personification gives a vivid impression of an object or place

The Prelude: Stealing the Boat (Pages 6-7)

1) The personification of the mountain makes it seem threatening — the phrase "Upreared its head" creates a monstrous image.
2) The personified mountain "Strode after" the narrator, giving a vivid sense that it means to harm him. Its calm but relentless pursuit increases his terror.

The Emigrée (Pages 26-27)

1) The city is initially personified as being "sick with tyrants", suggesting it has been damaged in some way.
2) However, in the third stanza, the city is personified positively. It returns to the speaker in a "white plane" and takes her "dancing" — this could reflect the vividness of the speaker's memories.
3) In the closing lines of the poem, the speaker's city "hides behind" her — the personification makes it sound as if the speaker has to defend her attachment to the city.

Similes and metaphors can be powerful ways of making a point

Remains (Pages 18-19)

1) The metaphor, "dug in behind enemy lines", describes the way that the speaker can't get the memory of the looter's death out of his mind — it emphasises the lasting effect the death has had on the speaker. It also highlights the continuing sense of threat that he feels from the memory.
2) The phrase "dug in" hints at how deeply the memory is embedded and that it won't be easily removed.

Poppies (Pages 20-21)

1) The simile describing the mother leaning against the war memorial "like a wishbone" reinforces her desperate wish for her son to return safely. Her leaning also hints that she's searching for some support.
2) Another simile is used to illustrate the son's excitement at leaving — "the world overflowing / like a treasure chest" gives a vivid sense of his anticipation and the varied, rich experiences he hopes for.

Checking Out Me History (Pages 30-31)

1) The speaker uses metaphors of blindness to emphasise the history hidden from him by his formal education. Plosive words like "Bandage" and "Blind" at the start of lines give the metaphors extra power.
2) In comparison, metaphors of light are used to describe the Caribbean heroes — e.g. "Toussaint" is a "beacon", while "Mary Seacole" is a "healing star" and a "yellow sunrise". These positive metaphors help reinforce the speaker's point that these figures are worthy of being studied.

Other poems also use personification...

Owen and Heaney both personify nature — in 'Exposure' it is personified as the enemy of the men, and in 'Storm on the Island' personification is used to make the storm seem more threatening and dangerous.

Rhyme and Rhythm

Rejoice happily, your teacher has marshmallows — there's no excuse for spelling 'rhythm' wrong in the exam.

1) Rhyme and rhythm affect the mood of a poem and how it flows.
2) They can also be used to create a particular effect or to emphasise the message of a poem.

Rhyme can reinforce a poem's message

London (Pages 4-5)

1) The regular ABAB rhyme scheme emphasises the unrelenting suffering and lack of change in the city.
2) The rhymes are simple and often monosyllabic (e.g. "street" and "meet"), giving the poem a strong beat. This could replicate the thudding sound of a heartbeat, presenting the city as mass of humanity.

My Last Duchess (Pages 8-9)

1) Rhyming couplets are used throughout the poem to help create a rigid form — this shows how the Duke controls the poem, just as he controlled his wife's fate.
2) The regularity of the rhymes also mirrors the Duke's stubborn, unwavering character — the rhyme scheme allows no space for change or questioning, just as the Duke chooses "Never to stoop".

Checking Out Me History (Pages 30-31)

1) 'Checking Out Me History' uses lots of rhyme but has no regular rhyme scheme. Agard uses rhyme differently in the British and Caribbean stanzas to emphasise his points about education and identity.
2) Lots of simple rhymes (e.g. "cat" and "dat") are used in the British quatrains. The rhymes sound childish and make the British history the speaker was taught seem trivial.
3) Rhyme is used less frequently and less regularly in the Caribbean stanzas. This reflects the speaker's wish for freedom from the restrictions of his formal education.

A poem's rhythm affects its pace and mood

The Charge of the Light Brigade (Pages 10-11)

1) The regular rhythm creates a sense of the energy and speed of the cavalry charging into battle. This sense of action and excitement also helps to emphasise the soldiers' heroism.
2) The metre is mainly dactylic — one stressed syllable is followed by two unstressed ones (e.g. "All in the valley of Death"). This creates a galloping effect, like the sound of the horses' hooves.

Bayonet Charge (Pages 16-17)

1) Enjambment, caesura and varying line lengths create an irregular rhythm that mirrors the soldier struggling and stumbling through the mud.
2) The lack of a regular rhythm also adds to the soldier's feeling of "bewilderment" and helplessness — there is no calmness or order that a regular rhythm may offer.

Rhyme schemes are important in other poems...

'Exposure' has a regular ABBAC rhyme scheme which contributes to the feeling of monotony and misery. In 'Ozymandias', the lack of a conventional rhyme scheme reflects how human power can be destroyed.

Voice

The voice is a key feature of a poem — it can have a big effect on how the poet's message is conveyed.

1) A first-person voice gives you one person's perspective.
2) Poetry can reproduce spoken language to hint at the speaker's character.

Using a first-person narrator makes the poem more personal

Poppies (Pages 20-21)

1) The use of the first person allows the poet to express the mother's memories and emotions, e.g. "I was brave". The narrator speaks personally and intimately, as if she is expressing her most private thoughts.
2) Domestic language and imagery gives the mother a unique voice. For example, she describes her nervousness with sewing imagery — "my stomach busy / making tucks, darts, pleats".

Kamikaze (Pages 28-29)

1) In the later stanzas, the voice switches to the direct speech of the pilot's daughter.
2) This signals a change of tone — the direct speech makes the poem more personal, but it also presents information in a more matter-of-fact way. This helps the reader to empathise with the daughter.

Poems can include features of spoken language

My Last Duchess (Pages 8-9)

1) The poem is written entirely in the Duke's voice. Interjections, e.g. "how shall I say?", and contractions, e.g. "'twas" and "Will't", give the sense that the Duke is speaking aloud.
2) Questions ("Will't please you rise?") and references to "Sir" show that the Duke is having a conversation. However, the fact that we only ever hear the Duke's voice emphasises his power and need for control.

Remains (Pages 18-19)

1) Armitage uses colloquial language (e.g. "legs it") and contractions (e.g. "I'm") to make the poem sound like a spoken account. The colloquial tone means that the looter's death is presented as an everyday event that's a normal part of the speaker's job.
2) Using the soldier's authentic voice helps the conflict to seem real and human, and gives the reader a deeper sense of the soldier's troubled mind.

Checking Out Me History (Pages 30-31)

1) Phonetic spellings (e.g. "Wha" and "dat") reflect the speaker's Caribbean accent — this shows that he is proud of his Caribbean heritage.
2) The speaker also uses non-standard grammar and broken syntax (e.g. "and first Black / Republic born"). This suggests that he wants to rebel against the standard English grammar he's been taught.
3) The phonetic spellings reinforce the speaker's anger, e.g. "Dem" is a more forceful sound than "They".

Third-person narrators are more removed from the action...

The narrator in 'War Photographer' is separate from the photographer, allowing the reader to observe him at a distance. The narrator of 'The Charge of the Light Brigade' is able to comment on the battle from afar.

Beginnings of Poems

Poets know that first impressions are important, so there's usually something to say about openings of poems.

1) The beginning of a poem often sets the tone for the rest of the poem.
2) Poets aim to draw in their readers, and to establish something of the poem's meaning.

Openings can be used to set the scene

Structure is the way that poets order and develop their ideas in a poem. The beginnings and endings of poems are key structural devices.

Exposure (Pages 12-13)

1) The opening phrase of 'Exposure', "Our brains ache", introduces the idea of pain and suffering, and also highlights the fact that this is a collective experience, shared by many soldiers.
2) "Our brains ache" is also a reference to "My heart aches" — the opening of 'Ode to a Nightingale' by John Keats, a 'Romantic' poet (see p.2). The 'Romantics' believed that nature could inspire and restore, so Owen's reference to Keats here seems ironic — nature in 'Exposure' is deadly.
3) The "winds" that "knive" the soldiers in the first line establish nature as an enemy.

Storm on the Island (Pages 14-15)

1) The opening of 'Storm on the Island' — "We are prepared:" — also hints at a collective experience. This contributes to the initial feeling of safety — the islanders seem to have strength and safety in numbers.
2) The first two lines have several further references to solidity, including "rock" and "good slate". Both lines are also end-stopped, which reinforces the sense of security.
3) However, the opening sets the scene for the arrival of the storm — the reader may question why the sturdiness of the buildings is emphasised and whether the confidence of the opening is justified.

Some openings use a structural device

Ozymandias (Pages 2-3)

1) The narrator only speaks for one line — the rest of the poem is the reported speech of the "traveller".
2) This creates a distance between the reader and Ozymandias — the reader only hears a second-hand account about Ozymandias, reducing the importance of the ruler.
3) The insignificance of Ozymandias is also shown by the fact that the traveller is "from an antique land". The word "antique" emphasises that the king has little relevance anymore.

Bayonet Charge (Pages 16-17)

1) The poem begins *in medias res* (in the middle of the action) — this puts the reader in a similarly confused position to the soldier who "awoke" to find himself in battle.
2) Starting the poem with the dramatic adverb, "Suddenly", establishes a sense of urgency and reflects the sense of panic that is present throughout the poem. It also grabs the reader's attention.
3) The soldier is already "running" as he wakes up — this makes his experience sound like a nightmare.

You can comment on the beginning of any poem...

'The Charge of the Light Brigade' begins with rhythmic repetition that immediately gives a sense of movement. 'Remains' and 'The Emigrée' both open with phrases that make them sound like stories.

Endings of Poems

Relief might be your emotion when you reach the end of a poem, but please don't write that in your exam...

1) Last lines can sum up or neatly round off a poem.
2) Poems often end with a powerful or memorable image.

Paul feared that the ending might not be as fun as the beginning.

Last lines can create a sense of finality...

My Last Duchess (Pages 8-9)

1) The focus at the end shifts back to the Duke's art collection — he points out his statue of "Neptune" and is keen to tell his visitor that "Claus of Innsbruck" made it for him, showing again his pride and vanity.
2) This confirms that, for the Duke, the story of his last Duchess is over — he has moved on and she is now just another possession in his art collection.

War Photographer (Pages 22-23)

1) 'War Photographer' ends with a rhyming couplet describing the photographer flying away from England, back to a war zone. He's leaving England and ending this chapter of his life.
2) Monosyllabic words are used to give emphasis to the closing phrase — "they do not care". The simple words hint that he's frustrated by the wider world's apathy about suffering elsewhere.

Tissue (Pages 24-25)

1) The ending sums up the speaker's ideas about the preciousness of life and the importance of heritage.
2) The final section of the poem (from line 25) builds up to the ending. It suggests that human beings — a "grand design" of "living tissue" — are more impressive and significant than other man-made structures.
3) The final line of the poem stands alone, which makes it seem significant. The line uses a direct address ("your skin"), which encourages the reader to consider their own heritage.

...or they can leave you with doubts

Bayonet Charge (Pages 16-17)

1) The final line ("His terror's touchy dynamite.") is ambiguous and makes the reader question the soldier's fate. Ending with "dynamite" implies danger, and the adjective "touchy" suggests an explosion is imminent.
2) The ending also feels sudden, just as the beginning does. The poem is a snapshot of this soldier's experience of war — the reader does not get a complete picture.

Kamikaze (Pages 28-29)

1) The poem ends with a return to the third-person voice and speculation about the pilot's feelings. The daughter will never know exactly how her father felt, and will always be full of regret and uncertainty.
2) The reader is also left wondering whether the pilot felt he made the right decision — there is no answer to the question of whether he wished he had fulfilled his suicide mission.

Other poems feature interesting endings...

'London', 'Exposure' and 'Remains' all end with particularly negative images that offer no hope of change or improvement. Similarly, 'The Prelude' and 'Storm on the Island' both end with fear of nature.

Mood

Sadly there are no teenage-angst poems in this cluster, but there's still plenty for you to write about moods.

1) The mood is the feeling or atmosphere created in a poem.
2) Poets often change the mood of the poem as it progresses.

Imagery can be used to create a specific mood

Exposure (Pages 12-13)

1) Bleak natural imagery reflects the hopeless, dejected mood of the soldiers.
2) Traditional poetic imagery is subverted to emphasise the grim nature of their experience. "Dawn" brings misery instead of hope, and the snow is "black" and "deathly" rather than white and pure. Even the "fires" of home are "crusted dark-red jewels" — they offer no warmth or comfort.
3) The repetition of "But nothing happens" also contributes to the tedious, monotonous mood. It confirms that there is little hope of the mood changing.

War Photographer (Pages 22-23)

1) Religious imagery in the first stanza creates a solemn mood. The similes comparing the darkroom to a "church", and the photographer to "a priest preparing to intone a Mass" make this sound like a funeral.
2) This mood endures throughout the poem — it emphasises the care the photographer takes over his work, his respect for the victims of the war and his sorrow at the suffering and loss of life his photographs depict.

"But I thought you liked puns."
"Stop it — I'm just not in the mood."

Some poems have a change in mood

The Prelude: Stealing the Boat (Pages 6-7)

1) At the start of the extract, the mood is mostly happy, light and carefree — the speaker seems confident and comfortable, and nature seems beautiful and tranquil.
2) However, the mood changes suddenly and completely with the line "When, from behind that craggy steep...". It becomes sinister and threatening as the mountain "Upreared its head" and "Strode after" the narrator, the personification emphasising its power and hostility.
3) The poem ends in a philosophical mood — the speaker reflects on the experience and his new understanding of nature's power.

Storm on the Island (Pages 14-15)

1) The poem is structured around the switch in mood from safety and security to fear and threat.
2) The confident opening of "We are prepared" is mirrored by the helpless "We are bombarded" in line 18 — the storm is uncontrollable and all the islanders can do is "just sit tight".
3) The poem ends with the word "fear" — this is the overriding emotion of the islanders.

'Remains' and 'The Emigrée' also have shifts in mood...

The laid-back, almost jovial mood at the start of 'Remains' changes when the speaker's guilt takes over. In 'The Emigrée', the speaker's nostalgic mood is challenged by people threatening her in the final stanza.

Practice Questions

It's the end of the section and yep, you guessed it — time for some questions to check if you've taken everything in. Try to answer them without looking back through the section — that's the best way to see if you're on the way to being a poetry pro.

Forms of Poetry

1) Explain how the form of 'War Photographer' mirrors the photographer's work.
2) Comment on the form of 'The Charge of the Light Brigade'. How does it reflect the chaos of war?
3) In 'Checking Out Me History', how does Agard use form to ridicule his British education?

Poetic Devices

1) Give an example of enjambment in 'Tissue' and explain its effect.
2) Give an example of repetition in 'Remains'. What effect does it have?
3) How does Shelley use irony in 'Ozymandias'? Does this influence your view of the king?
4) How does Garland use irony in 'Kamikaze' to make the pilot's fate seem tragic?
5) In 'London', how does Blake use appeals to the senses to emphasise the suffering in the city?
6) In 'The Emigrée', what is the effect of using the sense of taste in the second stanza?

Use of Sound

1) Do you think that the sounds of the battlefield are more realistic in 'Bayonet Charge' or 'The Charge of the Light Brigade'? Explain your answer.
2) Give some examples of repeated sounds in 'Exposure'. What effect do they have?
3) Give some examples of plosive words in 'Storm on the Island' and explain their effect.

Imagery

1) In 'The Prelude: Stealing the Boat', how does Wordsworth use personification to make the speaker's encounter seem more frightening?
2) In 'Poppies', how are similes used to show the contrasting emotions of the mother and her son?
3) Find a metaphor used to describe a Caribbean hero in 'Checking Out Me History'. Explain the meaning and significance of the metaphor.

Practice Questions

Rhyme and Rhythm

1) Describe the effect of the rhyming couplets used in 'My Last Duchess'.
2) Explain how Agard uses rhyme in 'Checking Out Me History' to emphasise the poem's message.
3) How does the rhythm of 'Bayonet Charge' contribute to the mood of the poem?

Voice

1) How does the first-person voice help the reader to empathise with the speaker in 'Poppies'?
2) In 'My Last Duchess', how does Browning create the impression of a conversation taking place?
3) What is the effect of the colloquial language in 'Remains'?

Beginnings of Poems

1) How does the beginning of 'Storm on the Island' show the islanders' state of mind?
2) Why do you think Shelley chose to only have the first line of 'Ozymandias' in the narrator's voice?
3) Choose a poem not mentioned on page 56 and write about the effect of its opening.

Endings of Poems

1) What does the ending of 'My Last Duchess' show you about the Duke's character?
2) Why do you think Dharker chose to separate the last line of 'Tissue' from the rest of the poem?
3) What is the effect of the last line of 'Bayonet Charge'? Do you think the soldier survived the war?

Mood

1) What is the mood in the final stanza of 'War Photographer'? Is this different from the first stanza?
2) What is the mood at the end of the extract from 'The Prelude'? How is this mood created?
3) What is the effect of the shift in mood in 'Storm on the Island'? What does the shift in mood suggest about the power of nature?

Practice Questions

Here's your third and final batch of exam-style questions. Sections Four and Five have lots of handy advice about writing a great exam answer, so have a read of those pages if you're looking for some hints and tips.

Exam-style Questions

1) Explore the ways in which individual experiences are portrayed in 'War Photographer' and one other poem from 'Power and Conflict'.

2) Compare the way that poets present memories in 'Remains' and one other poem from 'Power and Conflict'.

3) "A first-person narrator is the most effective way of conveying human emotions in a poem."

   Using this statement as a starting point, compare the use of narration in 'The Prelude: Stealing the Boat' and one other poem from 'Power and Conflict'.

4) Compare the way that the power of nature is presented in 'Storm on the Island' and in one other poem from 'Power and Conflict'.

5) "Striving for power is ultimately pointless."

   Using this statement as a starting point, compare the presentation of human power in 'Ozymandias' and one other poem from 'Power and Conflict'.

   Remember to comment on how the poems are written.

The Poetry Exam

If you're doing AQA English Literature, you'll have to sit two exams — this book will help you prepare for the Poetry Anthology section of Paper 2.

This is how your Paper 2 exam will work

1) The Paper 2 exam lasts for 2 hours and 15 minutes. It will be split into three sections, like this:

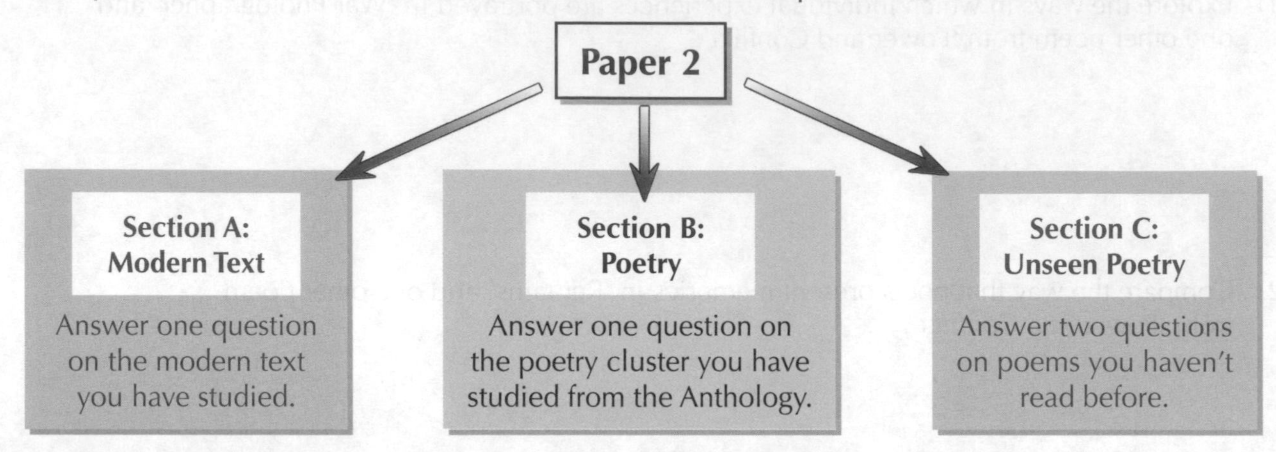

2) The next few pages give you tips on how to answer the question in Section B.
3) Section B has one question about each poetry cluster. You should only answer one of these questions — make sure you answer the question on the 'Power and Conflict' cluster.
4) Section B is worth 30 marks, which is about 20% of your entire GCSE. In the exam, you should spend about 45 minutes on Section B.
5) You're not allowed to take your own anthology or any notes about the poems into the exam.

Read the question carefully and underline key words

1) Read the question for 'Power and Conflict' carefully. Underline the theme and any other key words.
2) The question will give you one poem and ask you to compare it with any other poem from the same cluster. You'll be given a list of all the poems to help you choose — pick one that relates to the theme.
3) Here's the kind of question you'll get in the exam:

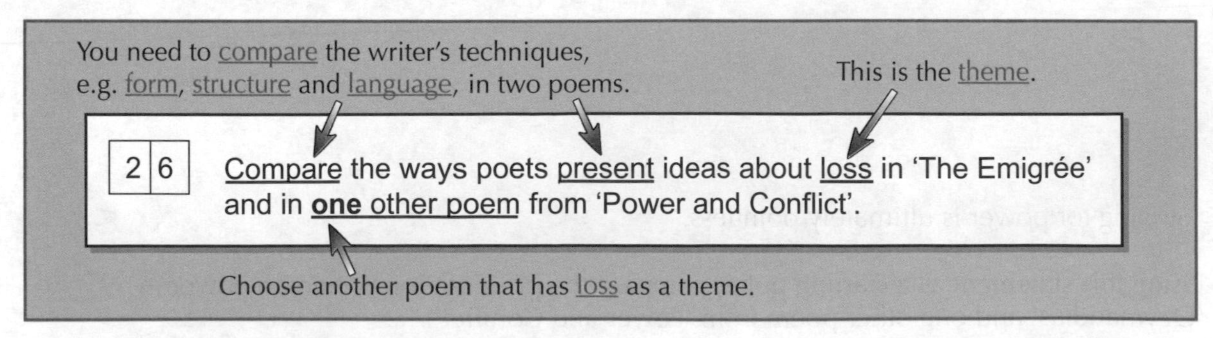

There are three main ways to get marks

There are three main things to keep in mind when you're planning and writing your answer:

- Give your own thoughts and opinions on the poems and support them with quotes from the text.
- Explain features like form, structure and language.
- Describe the similarities and differences between poems and their contexts.

How to Structure Your Answer

A solid structure is essential — it lets the examiner follow your argument nice and easily. The best way to make sure you write a well-structured essay in the exam is to make a plan before you start writing (see p.67).

Start with an introduction and end with a conclusion

1) Your introduction should begin by giving a clear answer to the question in a sentence or two. Use the rest of the introduction to briefly develop this idea — try to include some of the main ideas from your plan.
2) The main body of your essay should be three to five paragraphs that compare the two poems.
3) Finish your essay with a conclusion — this should summarise your answer to the question. It's also your last chance to impress the examiner, so try to make your final sentence memorable.

Compare the poems throughout your essay

1) In each paragraph of the main body, write about one poem and then explain whether the other poem is similar or different. Don't just write several paragraphs about one poem, followed by several paragraphs about the other.
2) Every paragraph should compare a feature of the poems, such as their form, their structure, the language they use or the feelings they put across.
3) Link your ideas with words like 'similarly', 'likewise' or 'equally' when you're writing about a similarity. Or use phrases such as 'in contrast' and 'on the other hand' if you're explaining a difference.

Remember to start a new paragraph every time you start comparing a new feature of the poems.

Use P.E.E.D. to structure each paragraph

1) P.E.E.D. stands for: Point, Example, Explain, Develop.

POINT — Begin each paragraph by making a comparison between the two poems.

EXAMPLE — Then give an example from one of the poems.

EXPLAIN — Explain how the example supports your opening point.

DEVELOP — Develop your point by writing about its effect on the reader, how it links to another part of the poem, how it relates to the poem's context, or by adding to the comparison with the other poem.

After you've explained your first example, give an example from the other poem and explain that too.

2) This is just a framework to make sure your paragraphs have all the features they need to pick up marks — you don't have to follow it rigidly in every paragraph.
3) Here's an example of how you could use P.E.E.D. to structure a paragraph:

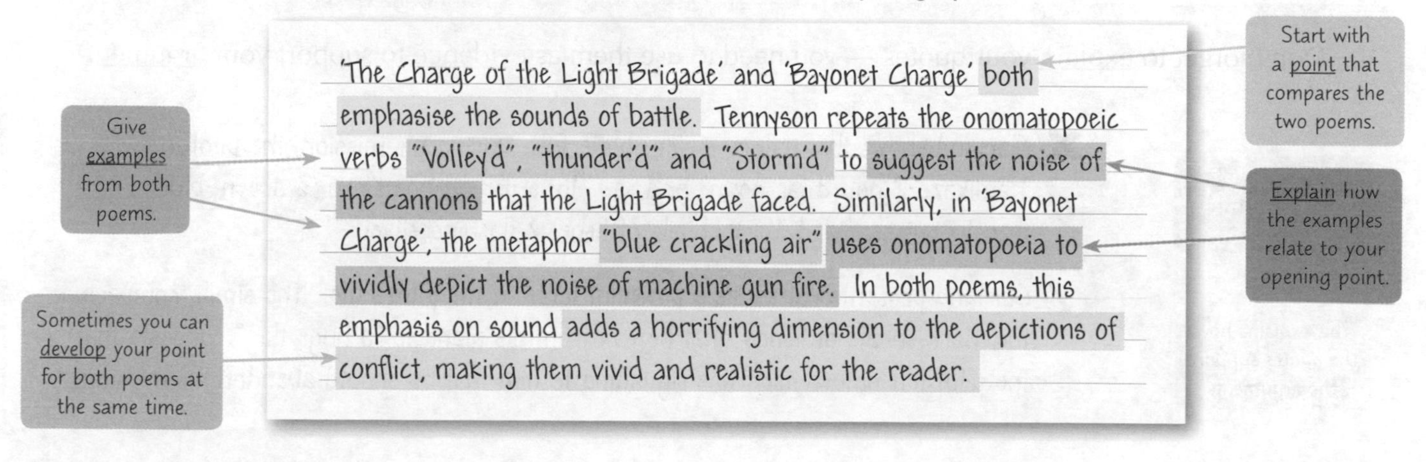

How to Answer the Question

The exam is no time to discover your inner politician — you actually need to answer the question you're given.

Look closely at language, form and structure

1) To get top marks, you need to pay close attention to the techniques the poets use.
2) Analyse the form and structure of the poems, which includes their rhyme scheme and rhythm.
3) Explore language — think about why the poets have used certain words and language techniques.
4) You also need to comment on the effect that these techniques have on the reader.
   The examiner wants to hear what you think of a poem and how it makes you feel.
5) This is the kind of thing you could write about language:

'Poppies' makes frequent references to the injury and bereavement caused by conflict. The poem opens with a reference to the poppies placed "on individual war graves". By emphasising the personal, individual loss that conflict can cause, Weir highlights the narrator's fear that her own son will be killed in battle. The narrator's anxiety about the violence of conflict is further suggested by the depiction of poppy petals as "spasms of paper red". This metaphor evokes a vivid image of the physical injury that the narrator fears her son may suffer as a soldier, which helps the reader to understand the narrator's fears and to empathise with her. In contrast...

Analyse the effects of key quotes.

Always develop your ideas.

Always support your ideas with details from the text

1) To get top marks, you need to back up your ideas with quotes from or references to the text.
2) Choose your quotes carefully — they have to be relevant to the point you're making.
3) Don't quote large chunks of text — instead, use short quotes and embed them in your sentences.

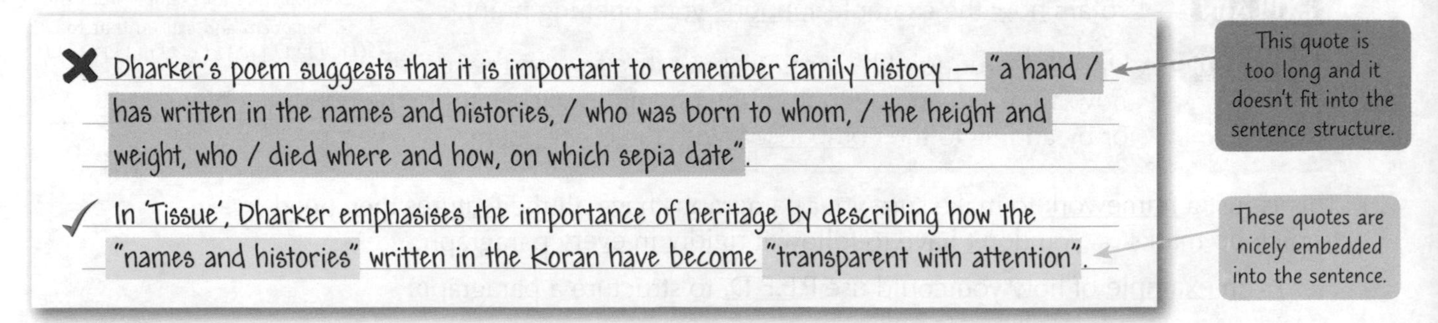

✗ Dharker's poem suggests that it is important to remember family history — "a hand / has written in the names and histories, / who was born to whom, / the height and weight, who / died where and how, on which sepia date".

This quote is too long and it doesn't fit into the sentence structure.

✓ In 'Tissue', Dharker emphasises the importance of heritage by describing how the "names and histories" written in the Koran have become "transparent with attention".

These quotes are nicely embedded into the sentence.

4) Don't forget to explain your quotes — you need to use them as evidence to support your argument.

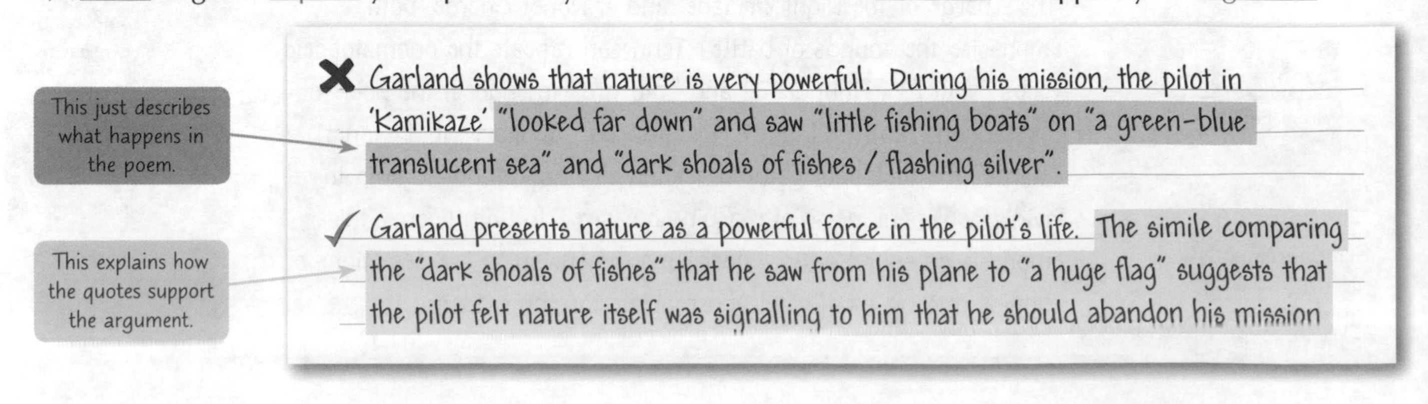

✗ Garland shows that nature is very powerful. During his mission, the pilot in 'Kamikaze' "looked far down" and saw "little fishing boats" on "a green-blue translucent sea" and "dark shoals of fishes / flashing silver".

This just describes what happens in the poem.

✓ Garland presents nature as a powerful force in the pilot's life. The simile comparing the "dark shoals of fishes" that he saw from his plane to "a huge flag" suggests that the pilot felt nature itself was signalling to him that he should abandon his mission

This explains how the quotes support the argument.

How to Answer the Question

The examiner doesn't have a list of right and wrong answers for this exam — you'll get plenty of marks for original or creative interpretations of the poems, as long as they're relevant and your points are developed well.

Give alternative interpretations

1) You need to show you're aware that poems can be interpreted in more than one way.
2) If a poem is a bit ambiguous, or you think that a particular line or phrase could have several different meanings, then say so.

> Some of the language used in 'The Emigrée' seems to suggest that the "city" is a real place: in the second stanza, the narrator refers to its "white streets" and "graceful slopes". However, other parts of the poem imply that the "city" may not be a physical place at all, but may symbolise a person, time or emotion that the narrator has lost. This interpretation is supported by the depiction of the "city" in the final stanza, when it is personified as a being that has "shining eyes" and "lies down in front of" the narrator.

Remember to support your interpretations with evidence from the poem.

3) Be original with your ideas — just make sure you can back them up with an example from the text.

Show some wider knowledge

1) To get a top grade, you need to explain how the ideas in the poems relate to their context.
2) When you're thinking about a particular poem, consider these aspects of context:

Historical — Do the ideas in the poem relate to the time in which it's written or set?

Geographical — How is the poem shaped and influenced by the place in which it's set?

Social — Is the poet criticising or praising the society or community they're writing about?

Cultural — Does the poet draw on a particular aspect of their background or culture?

Literary — Was the poet influenced by other works of literature or a particular literary movement?

3) Here are a couple of examples of how you might use context in your answer:

> Agard uses repetition and phonetic spellings in 'Checking Out Me History' to link the poem to the traditions of oral poetry. Oral recitation of poetry and history is common in the Caribbean, so by using these techniques, Agard is affirming his Caribbean roots and identity.

> The first words of 'Exposure', "Our brains ache", reference the opening of John Keats's poem, 'Ode to a Nightingale' — "My heart aches". This highlights the way that 'Romantic' ideals about nature have been destroyed by war. For the soldiers in the trenches, nature is an enemy rather than anything beautiful or inspirational.

How to Answer the Question

It's not just what you write that gets you a top grade, it's how you write it. Your writing style should be clear and precise, and you need to use the correct terms to show the examiner you know what you're talking about.

Use sophisticated language

1) Your writing has to sound sophisticated and stylish.

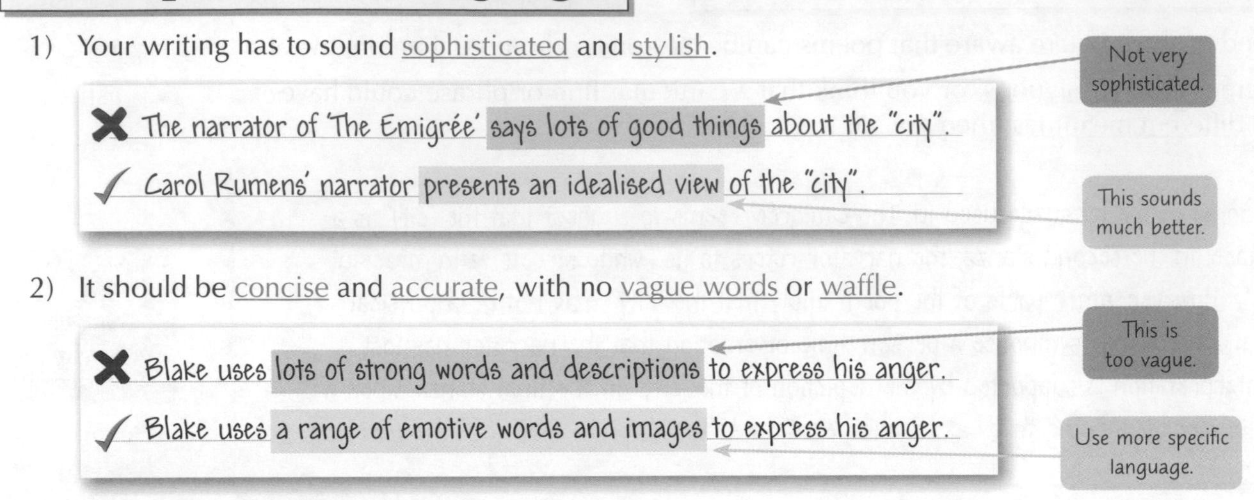

2) It should be concise and accurate, with no vague words or waffle.

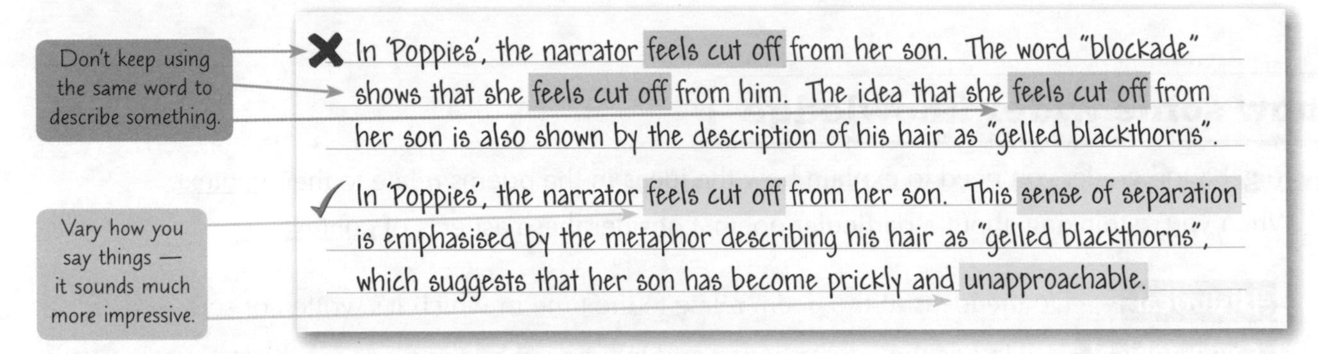

3) Your writing should also show an impressive range of vocabulary.

Don't keep using the same word to describe something.

✗ In 'Poppies', the narrator feels cut off from her son. The word "blockade" shows that she feels cut off from him. The idea that she feels cut off from her son is also shown by the description of his hair as "gelled blackthorns".

✓ In 'Poppies', the narrator feels cut off from her son. This sense of separation is emphasised by the metaphor describing his hair as "gelled blackthorns", which suggests that her son has become prickly and unapproachable.

Vary how you say things — it sounds much more impressive.

4) However, make sure you only use words that you know the meaning of. For example, don't say that a poem has a 'volta' if you don't know what it really means — it will be obvious to the examiner.

Use technical terms where possible

1) To get top marks, you need to use the correct technical terms when you're writing about poetry.
2) There's a handy glossary at the back of this book that explains these terms.

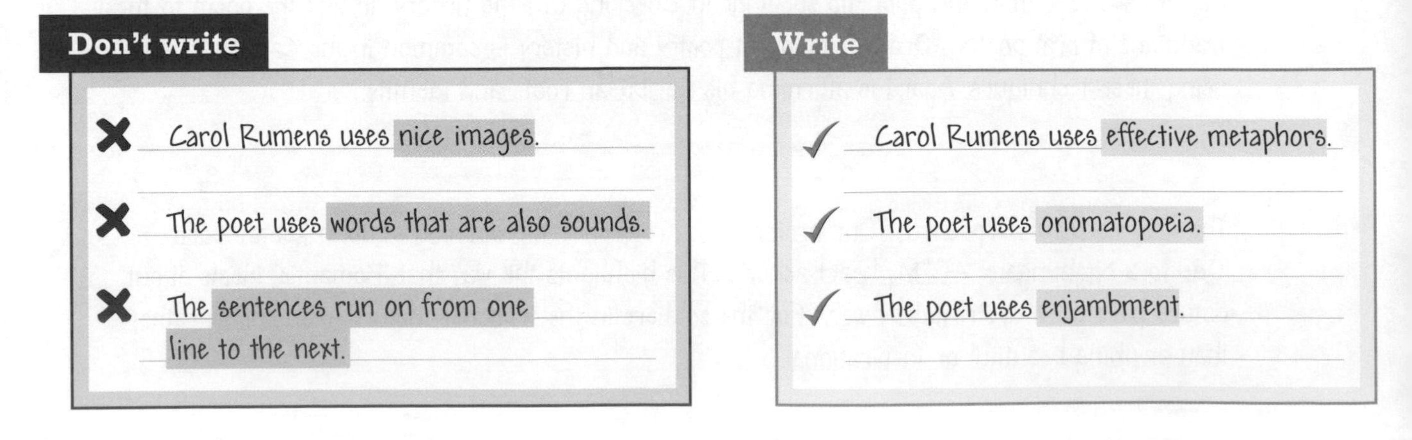

Planning Your Answer

In an exam, it's always tempting to launch straight into writing your answer, but that can end in disaster. Making a plan is the key to a sophisticated, well-structured essay. Trust me — it's worth it.

In the exam, spend five minutes planning your answer

1) Always plan your answer before you start writing — that way, you're less likely to forget something important.
2) Write your plan at the top of your answer booklet and draw a neat line through it when you've finished.
3) Don't spend too long on your plan. It's only rough work, so you don't need to write in full sentences. Here are a few examples of different ways you can plan your answer:

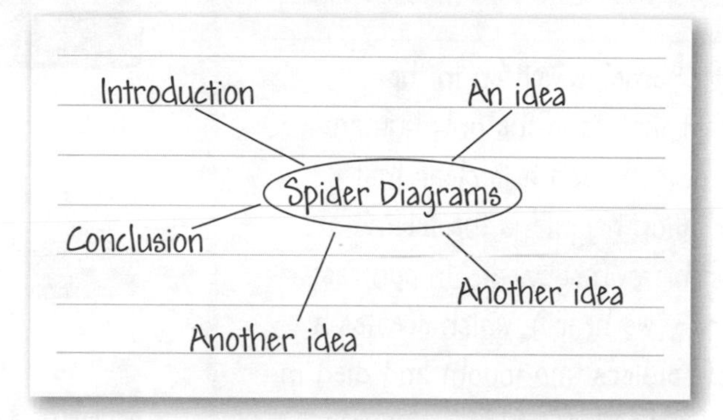

Bullet points with...
- Intro...
- An idea...
- The next idea...

Tables with...

A point...	Quote to back this up...
Another point...	Quote...
A different point...	Quote...

4) A good plan will help you organise your ideas — and write a good, well-structured essay.

Here's a sample question and plan

2 6 Compare the way poets present the reality of conflict in 'Bayonet Charge' and in **one** other poem from 'Power and Conflict'. **[30 marks]**

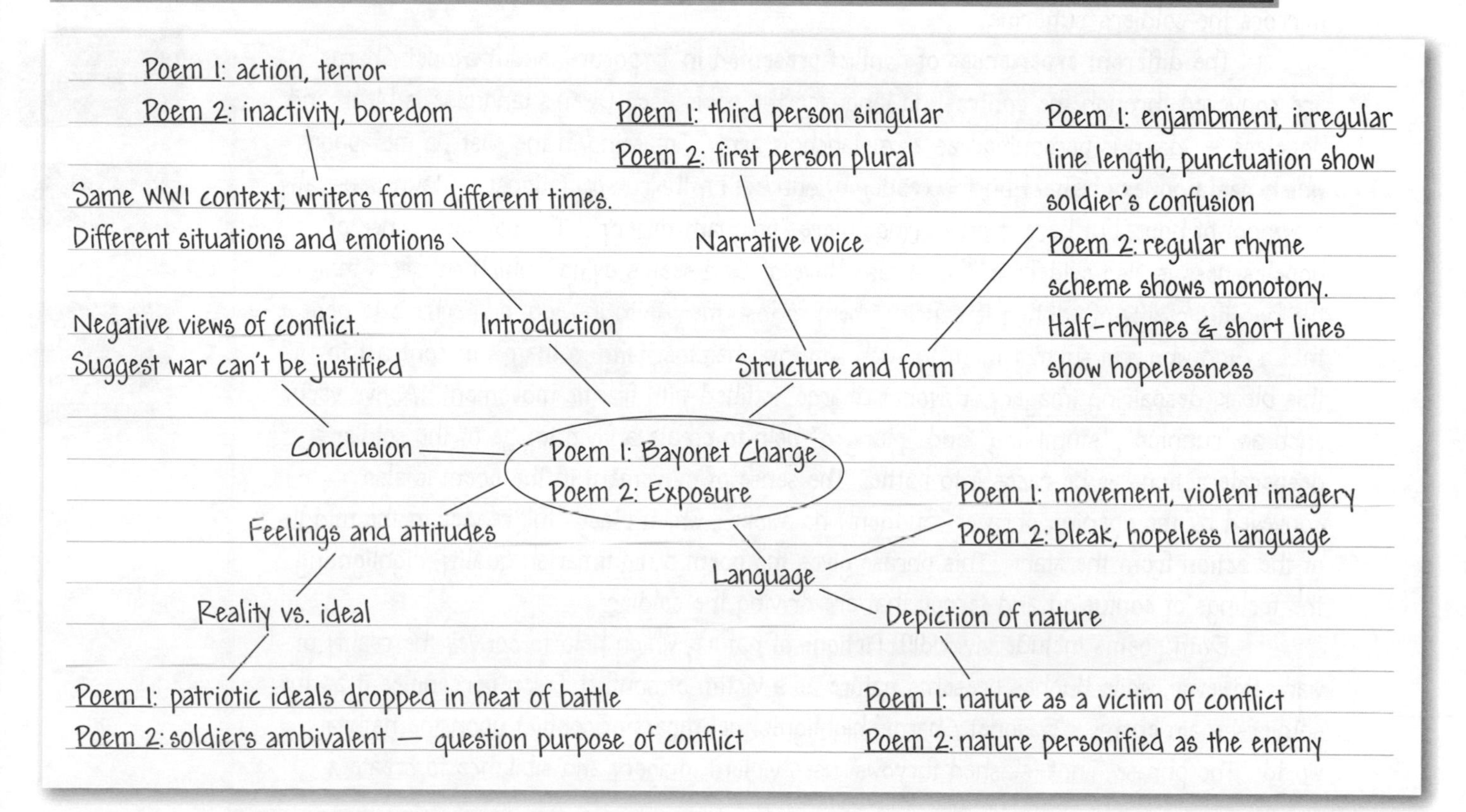

Sample Answer

Here's how you could use the plan on page 67 to write a really good answer.

Although the action of both 'Bayonet Charge' and 'Exposure' occurs on the battlefields of World War One, the poems offer two very different portrayals of the reality of conflict. While 'Bayonet Charge' depicts the violent action and overwhelming terror experienced by a soldier going into battle, 'Exposure' focuses on the boredom and inactivity of men waiting in the freezing trenches of the Western Front while "nothing happens" on the battlefield. Both poets present war as a profoundly negative experience, in which hope, faith and sense of self are overpowered by pain and fear.

Compare the poems in your opening sentence.

Sum up the main argument of your essay.

The poems use different narrative voices. 'Bayonet Charge' is written in the third person. The anonymity of the subject, "he", and the fact that he is the only human mentioned in the poem make him seem isolated and alone, even though it is clear that he must be surrounded by other soldiers. This sense of isolation heightens the feeling of terror in the poem by reflecting the soldier's acute focus on his own survival. In contrast, 'Exposure' is written in the first person plural ("our memory", "we hear"), which creates a sense of the shared suffering experienced by the millions of soldiers who fought and died in the First World War. This emphasises the vast scale of misery and loss of life in the war.

Try to develop your ideas.

The poets also use other aspects of form and structure to present the reality of conflict. In 'Bayonet Charge', Hughes uses enjambment and uneven line lengths to create an irregular rhythm, echoing the confusion experienced by the soldier. The irregular rhythm is heightened by caesurae in lines 11 and 15. These help to turn the second stanza into a pause in the action, which reflects the soldier's experience of time apparently standing still as he struggles to understand "the reason / Of his still running". In contrast, Owen uses a regular rhyme scheme (ABBAC) to emphasise the monotony experienced by the soldiers. Despite this regularity, half-rhymes such as "wire" / "war" create a sense of jarring discomfort that mirrors the soldiers' suffering.

Compare the poems' form and structure.

Use the correct technical terms.

Use examples to support your argument.

The different experiences of conflict presented in 'Exposure' and 'Bayonet Charge' are conveyed through the contrasting language the poets use. Owen's language is bleak and hopeless — dawn is personified as a "melancholy army" "massing in the east", a metaphor which has a powerful effect on the reader by subverting their expectations — dawn is usually a symbol of hope, but here it only brings more "poignant misery". The soldiers' sense of hopelessness is also evident in the phrase "love of God seems dying", which suggests that the horrific reality of conflict is causing them to lose their faith in God, or perhaps to believe that a God who can subject them to such suffering has lost faith in them. In contrast to this bleak, despairing imagery, 'Bayonet Charge' is filled with frantic movement. Active verbs such as "running", "stumbling" and "plunged" help to create a vivid image of the soldier's desperate actions as he races into battle. The sense of movement in the poem is also conveyed by the opening phrase, "Suddenly he awoke", which places the reader in the middle of the action from the start. This phrase gives the poem a nightmarish quality, highlighting the feelings of confusion and terror that are driving the soldier.

Compare the language used in the two poems.

Give a personal response.

Suggest more than one interpretation of the poem.

Both poems include vivid descriptions of nature, which help to convey the reality of war. However, while Hughes presents nature as a victim of conflict, Owen personifies it as the soldiers' main enemy. 'Bayonet Charge' highlights the impact of conflict upon the natural world. The phrase "shot-slashed furrows" uses violent imagery and sibilance to create a

Sample Answer

vivid picture of the damage that conflict does to the environment. Similarly, the distressing image of a "yellow hare" crawling "in a threshing circle" powerfully demonstrates the way that nature suffers at the hands of war. The image of the hare with "its mouth wide / Open silent" also symbolises the overwhelming, inexpressible fear experienced by the soldier as he runs into battle. In contrast, nature is personified as an enemy in 'Exposure', for example, its "merciless iced east winds" "knive" the soldiers. The sibilance in this metaphor reflects the sound of the wind and the sharp pain that it causes the men. Throughout the poem, this personification of nature highlights the danger that the soldiers are in and creates a bitter sense of irony — although the men are fighting in a war, the greatest danger they face is nature rather than any human force or army.

Both poems suggest that the reality of conflict does not match up to the ideal. In 'Bayonet Charge', Hughes questions the patriotic ideals of "King, honour, human dignity, etcetera", arguing that in the heat of battle they are "Dropped like luxuries" as terror takes over. Information about the horrors of World War One was readily available in the 1950s when Hughes wrote this poem, and there is a sense of pity for the soldiers who fought. Similarly, in 'Exposure', the narrator questions whether anything is achieved by the soldiers' sacrifice. On the surface, the phrase "Since we believe not otherwise can kind fires burn" suggests the soldiers believe their sacrifice is necessary to protect the "kind fires" of home, but the complex, broken syntax reflects their lack of conviction that this is true. This reveals the sense of alienation many soldiers felt: they believed no-one at home appreciated their sacrifice.

'Bayonet Charge' and 'Exposure' both present vividly negative views of the reality of conflict for soldiers on the front line. The experience of the soldiers in the two poems is very different: Hughes focuses on the raw terror and active suffering of a soldier going into battle, whereas Owen concentrates on the hopelessness and passive suffering of men dying from exposure. However, both poets use structure, form and vivid imagery to powerfully convey the soldiers' suffering. Both narrators question the patriotic ideals used to justify war, suggesting instead that there can be no justification for the bleak and dehumanising reality of conflict.

Use quotes to support your argument.

Explain the effect of the examples you give.

Start your paragraphs with a comparison.

Bring in some contextual details to your answer.

Your last sentence should sum up your argument, and it needs to be memorable.

How to write a top grade answer

There's no single way of getting a grade 9, but these handy hints will help you on your way:

1) Be original — examiners get bored of reading the same thing over and over again, so coming up with your own interpretations will impress them (as long as you can back up your ideas with evidence).
2) Be critical — this means giving your own opinions about the poems. For example:

> The phrase "poignant misery of dawn" compels the reader to experience the scene as the men in the trenches do: a bleak, melancholic landscape, devoid of hope and at the mercy of the elements.

3) Get to grips with context. It's not enough just to mention a link to context — you need to really explore the effect it has on the poem, or on your understanding of it. For example:

> Blake supported the French Revolution, in which the ruling classes were overthrown. This raises the question of whether his heavy use of rhetoric in 'London' may have been intended to persuade British citizens to stage a similar revolution.

Adding Quotes and Developing Points

The next couple of pages will give you a chance to practise your P.E.E.D. skills by adding quotes and developing the points in some sample answers. Enjoy...

You can find the answers for this section on p.80.

Complete this plan by adding quotes and developing points

1) Below is an exam question and a plan for answering it.
2) Find quotes from the poems to back up each of the language points in the table (marked **A**, **B**, **C** and **D**).
3) Make brief notes on your personal response to each poem (marked **E** and **F**) to complete the plan.

> 0 1 Compare the ways in which power is presented in 'Ozymandias' and in **one** other poem from 'Power and Conflict'. **[30 marks]**

	Ozymandias	My Last Duchess
Themes and ideas	Power of man insignificant compared to power of time/nature.	Duke's obsession with power over people and objects.
Language	Arrogant language ... **(A)** Irony ... **(B)**	Objectification of Duchess ... **(C)** Sinister language ... **(D)**
Form and Structure	Second-hand account. Sonnet with irregular rhyme scheme.	Dramatic monologue. Rhyming couplets. Enjambment.
Personal Response	**(E)**	**(F)**

Add quotes to improve these answers

In the sample answers below, replace each letter (**A**, **B** and **C**) with a suitable quote.

> 0 2 Compare how poets present the effects of conflict in 'Remains' and in **one** other poem from 'Power and Conflict'. **[30 marks]**

Answer Extract 1

'Remains' and 'War Photographer' both use powerful imagery to show the suffering that conflict brings to those living in war zones. In 'Remains', Armitage uses violent imagery, such as **(A)**, to convey the horror of the looter's death. The metaphorical description of the looter as **(B)** emphasises his suffering. Similarly, in 'War Photographer', the graphic description of **(C)** creates an emotive image of the suffering conflict causes. This has a powerful and disturbing effect on the reader, who has probably never experienced life in these war-torn places.

Answer Extract 2

Armitage suggests that the soldier resents the way that conflict has affected him. His haunting memories are emphasised by the repetition of **(A)** which emphasises his frustration at the situation. The frustrated tone of 'Remains' contrasts with the religious language used in 'War Photographer', which compares the photographer to **(B)**. This gives the poem a solemn tone, while the metaphor **(C)** suggests that the experience of conflict has made the photographer aware of the fragility of human life, rather than making him angry.

Adding Quotes and Developing Points

Have a go at developing these answers

1) Here are some more sample answers to question 2 on p.70.
2) In these extracts, the sentences followed by a letter (**A** or **B**) need to be developed further. Write an extra sentence to develop each point.

Remember — to develop your point you can write about its effect on the reader, how it links to another part of the poem, or how it relates to the poem's context.

0	2	Compare how poets present the effects of conflict in 'Remains' and in **one** other poem from 'Power and Conflict'. **[30 marks]**

Answer Extract 1

Armitage and Duffy both suggest that those who experience conflict are left with powerful memories that continue to affect them even after leaving the war zone. In 'Remains', the metaphor of the looter as being "dug in behind enemy lines" conveys the way that the memory of the shooting is still deeply embedded in the soldier's mind. **(A)**. The photographer in Duffy's poem is also left with terrible memories: the sensory memory of "the cries / of this man's wife" creates an emotive image of a family torn apart by war. **(B)**.

Answer Extract 2

Both poems use form to help illustrate the effects of conflict on their subjects. The uneven line lengths and lack of rhyme in 'Remains' give the poem an irregular rhythm, which mirrors the soldier's confusion and the way that he hasn't been able to return to a normal life. **(A)**. 'War Photographer', in contrast, has less variation in line lengths, and the poem has a regular ABBCDD rhyme scheme. This makes the poem seem calm and ordered, reflecting the photographer's way of coping with his experiences of conflict. **(B)**.

Answer Extract 3

The subjects of 'Remains' and 'War Photographer' both seem to be affected more deeply by their experiences of conflict once they return home. The soldier in 'Remains' is haunted by guilt for his part in the killing of the looter. Repetition of the phrase "probably armed, possibly not" reflects the way that the soldier replays the shooting in his own mind. **(A)**. Similarly, the photographer's hands "did not tremble" in the war zone, but "seem to now". This suggests that he was calm when confronted with the dangers of war, but physical symptoms of stress and trauma emerged later. **(B)**.

Mark Scheme

Over the next few pages, you're going to put your examiner's hat on (I know, it's a dream come true) and mark some sample answers. This will help you to see what you need to do to get a great mark in your exam.

This section gets you to mark a range of sample answers

1) Marking sample exam answers is a great way to find out exactly what you need to do in the exam to get the grade you want.
2) Most of the answers in this section are only extracts, not full answers. The essay you'll write in the exam will be longer — more like the one on pages 75-76.
3) The mark scheme below is similar to the one that the examiners will use to mark your exam answers.
4) Read the mark scheme thoroughly and make sure that you understand everything.
5) Once you understand the mark scheme, use it to mark the sample exam answers on the next few pages. Don't forget to explain why you chose each grade.

Use this mark scheme to mark the sample answers

Grade band	What is written
8-9	• Shows an insightful and original comparison of the two poems • Effectively integrates a full range of precise examples to support interpretations • Closely analyses the poets' use of language, structure and form, making effective use of technical terms throughout • Gives a detailed exploration of how the poets' techniques affect the reader • Convincingly explores original and alternative interpretations of the ideas, themes, attitudes and context of the poems
6-7	• Presents a carefully thought out, developed comparison of the two poems • Integrates well-chosen examples to support interpretations • Explores the poets' use of language, structure and form, using correct technical terms • Examines the way the techniques used in the poems affect the reader • Gives careful consideration to the ideas, themes, attitudes and/or context of the poems, offering some original interpretations
4-5	• Gives a clear comparison of the two poems • Provides relevant detail to support interpretations of the poems • Explains how the poets have used some features of language, structure and form, using some relevant technical terms • Comments on how some of the techniques used in the poems affect the reader • Shows a clear understanding of the ideas, themes, attitudes and/or context of the poems

You can also be awarded grades 1-3. We haven't included any sample answer extracts at 1-3 level though — so those grades aren't in this mark scheme.

Marking Answer Extracts

Here's your first set of sample answers. For each one, think about where it fits in the mark scheme on page 72. Most answers won't fit the criteria for any one band exactly — it's about finding the best fit.

Have a go at marking these answer extracts

For each extract:

a) Write down the grade band (4-5, 6-7 or 8-9) you think the answer falls into.

b) Give at least two reasons why you chose that grade band.

> **0 3** Compare the ways the poets present negative feelings in 'London' and in **one** other poem from 'Power and Conflict'. **[30 marks]**

Answer Extract 1

'London' and 'Checking Out Me History' both use language to present negative feelings. In 'London', the narrator uses phrases like "every infant's cry" to show why London makes him angry. He also describes the church and the palace in negative ways, for example "black'ning church", to show that he is angry with them. In 'Checking Out Me History', the narrator shows that he is angry with British society by making British history sound unimportant ("all dat"), and by repeating the words "Dem tell me".

Answer Extract 2

Both poets use imagery to convey their anger at authority. In 'London', the phrase "black'ning church" suggests the churches are literally blackened by soot, but also hints that the speaker considers the Church to be rotten and corrupt. The emotive reference in the previous line to the crying "chimney-sweeper", a victim of child labour, suggests that the church is morally 'blackened' by its failure to help the poor and exploited. Similarly, Agard uses metaphors such as "Bandage up me eye" and "Blind me" to express the narrator's resentment of his formal education. The pairing of "Bandage" and "Blind me" creates a sense of irony — the bandage has blinded the narrator rather than healing him. This irony underscores the narrator's bitterness about the way his formal education caused him to lose his "history" and his "identity".

Answer Extract 3

Both poets use repetition to emphasise their anger. In 'London', Blake repeats the words "mark" and "every". This emphasises the feelings of despair that the narrator senses in "every face" he meets in London, which helps the reader understand why the situation in the city upsets him. Similarly, in 'Checking Out Me History', the repetition of the phrase "Dem tell me" throughout the poem makes the narrator sound angry and frustrated. It also demonstrates the narrator's sense of alienation from the education system, "Dem". This helps to present his frustration to the reader in a clear way.

Marking Answer Extracts

You must be getting the hang of this now — if you get much more practice you'll be putting those English examiners out of a job. Remember to look out for comparison of the two poems in these extracts.

Have a go at marking these answer extracts

Remember to keep looking back at the mark scheme on page 72.

For each extract:

a) Write down the grade band (4-5, 6-7 or 8-9) you think the answer falls into.

b) Give at least two reasons why you chose that grade band.

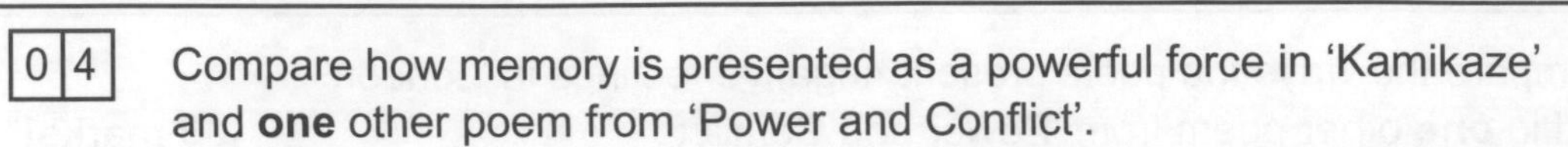

0 4 Compare how memory is presented as a powerful force in 'Kamikaze' and **one** other poem from 'Power and Conflict'. **[30 marks]**

Answer Extract 1

Powerful memories significantly influence the actions of both the pilot in 'Kamikaze' and the speaker in 'The Emigrée'. The speaker in 'Kamikaze' suggests that the pilot chose to turn his plane around after remembering waiting for his "father's boat" to return "safe" from fishing trips. The subsequent repetition of "safe" hints that the pilot cannot bring himself to complete his suicide mission as it will mean that his children are left without a father. Repetition is also used to show the power of memories in 'The Emigrée' — the word "sunlight" is repeated at the end of each stanza, which shows how the speaker maintains her positive view of her city despite the threats she and the city face. The repetition of words in both poems reflects the repetition of memories in the characters' minds, highlighting the enduring power that memories have.

Answer Extract 2

The pilot in 'Kamikaze' and the speaker in 'The Emigrée' both have happy memories of their childhoods which affect them as adults. In 'Kamikaze', the pilot's memories make him turn his plane around. He remembers playing with his brothers — they built "cairns of pearl-grey pebbles". This is why he didn't want to die in the war. In 'The Emigrée', the speaker has happy memories of where she lived as a child. She says that her memories of it are "sunlight-clear" which shows that they are positive memories and they are still clear to her. She also says that her "original view" of the city "cannot break", showing that they are also strong memories.

Answer Extract 3

Both poets present memory as a powerful force that shapes and influences individuals. In 'Kamikaze', the "powerful incantations" of patriotic messages that fill the pilot's head are replaced by idyllic childhood memories, including awaiting the "safe" arrival of his "father's boat", which foreshadows the pilot's safe landing of his plane. It is these enduring, formative memories that direct the pilot's actions — not the Japanese propaganda. The speaker in 'The Emigrée' has memories that are so vivid that they are personified, appearing to her and even taking her "dancing". This personification emphasises the power that her positive memories hold — they are so powerful that they materialise in a physical form that she engages and interacts with. In both instances, childhood memories are shown to have tangible impact on adult characters, influencing their actions and moods

Marking a Whole Answer

New page, new question and answer. Only this time it's the whole answer, not just an extract...

Now try marking this whole answer

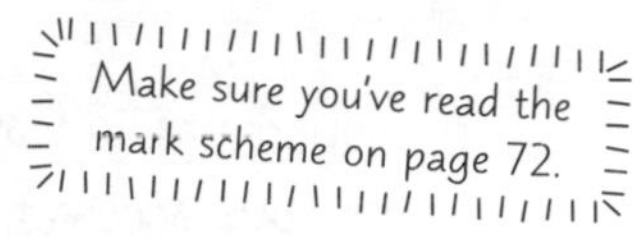

a) Write down the grade band (4-5, 6-7 or 8-9) you think the answer falls into.

b) Give at least four reasons why you chose that grade band.

| 0 | 5 | Compare how poets present the power of nature in 'The Prelude: Stealing the Boat' and in **one** other poem from 'Power and Conflict'. **[30 marks]**

'The Prelude: Stealing the Boat' and 'Storm on the Island' both present nature as a powerful force which can have a profound effect on humans. In Wordsworth's poem, the narrator experiences nature's power when he sees a "huge" mountain while rowing "A little boat" on a lake, while in Heaney's poem an island community experiences the violent power of nature in the form of a great storm that "pummels" them. Both poems present nature as having power over humans — in Heaney's poem the impact of this power is physical, whereas in Wordsworth's poem it is psychological.

Wordsworth and Heaney both use personification to present nature as a dominant force that can threaten humans. Wordsworth's narrator describes how the mountain "Strode after" him with "measured motion". The word "measured" and the use of alliteration in this phrase emphasise nature's power by making it sound as if the mountain is moving deliberately and unstoppably towards the narrator. The suggestion that the mountain is chasing the narrator makes it seem threatening, and enables the reader to share in the narrator's fear. Heaney also personifies nature, using language usually associated with war, such as "strafes" and "bombarded" to describe the actions of the wind. The use of such violent imagery emphasises the power of the storm, and suggests that the wind is deliberately attacking the island. This highlights how destructive the storm could be, which helps to clarify the islanders' fear.

In both poems, the sense of threat caused by nature's power is heightened by the use of contrasting imagery. In Wordsworth's poem, the "grim shape" of the mountain contrasts with pretty images such as "sparkling light", which are used to describe nature in the first 20 lines. This contrast emphasises the power of the mountain, and increases the sense of fear after the narrator encounters it. Heaney also uses contrast to intensify feelings of fear. For example, the simile comparing the sea during the storm to "a tame cat / Turned savage" juxtaposes a safe image with a violent one to show that the storm has the power to make even familiar things seem frightening. The enjambment across these lines places emphasis on "Turned", making nature's transformation from familiar to terrifying seem even more sudden and shocking.

Both poems have a distinct turning point, which makes the power of nature seem more dramatic. In 'The Prelude: Stealing the Boat', the volta in line 21 represents the moment when the narrator first encounters the "huge peak", and at this point the mood of the poem shifts from

This answer continues on page 76.

Marking a Whole Answer

confidence to fear. For example, in line 12 the narrator describes himself as "Proud of his skill" as he rows across the lake, which makes him sound confident and perhaps even arrogant. In contrast, after seeing the mountain, he becomes fearful and preoccupied — he rows with "trembling oars", and is "in grave / And serious mood". The suddenness of this shift from confidence to fear emphasises the dramatic impact that the power of nature has on the narrator. Similarly, in 'Storm on the Island', the volta in line 14 represents the arrival of the storm. The language used after this turning point, such as "We just sit tight", emphasises the islanders' lack of power, which contrasts with the poem's confident opening statement, "We are prepared". As in Wordsworth's poem, this change of tone emphasises nature's power over humans, suggesting that, despite all their preparations, the island community is powerless in the face of the storm.

Both poets use other aspects of form and structure to reinforce their depictions of nature's power over humans. In the final 10 lines of 'The Prelude: Stealing the Boat', which describe how the encounter with the mountain continued to affect the narrator "for many days", Wordsworth uses caesurae and enjambment to break up the sentences — "No familiar shapes / Remained, no pleasant images of trees." These fractured sentences reflect the narrator's feelings of confusion as he struggles to make sense of his experience, demonstrating the powerful effect that nature has had on him. In 'Storm on the Island', Heaney uses a caesura in line 14, just before the arrival of the storm. This sudden pause represents the calm before the storm, and creates a sense of expectation, reflecting the islanders' anxiety as they wait for the storm to arrive. The caesura also reflects the way that life stops when a storm comes, as people "sit tight", waiting for it to pass. This highlights the extent to which the islanders' lives are controlled by nature.

Both poems emphasise the physical presence of nature in order to highlight its power. In 'The Prelude: Stealing the Boat', Wordsworth repeats the word "huge" in the phrase "a huge peak, black and huge" to emphasise the mountain's size, suggesting that its physical appearance seemed overwhelming to the narrator. In common with other Romantic poets, Wordsworth suggests that nature has a formative effect on human identity: it is this experience of nature's visible, domineering physical presence that has such a lasting psychological impact on the narrator, with "huge and mighty forms" haunting him day and night. In contrast, in 'Storm on the Island', Heaney focuses on the invisibility of the winds that seem to attack the island — "We are bombarded by the empty air". This paradox of the storm's violent but invisible physical power emphasises the islanders' powerlessness in the face of the storm, showing that it is impossible for them to fight back against the "huge nothing" that assaults them. This realistic portrayal of nature as a powerful physical force is informed by Heaney's childhood: growing up on a farm in rural Northern Ireland meant that nature played an important role in his life.

Despite being written more than a century apart, 'The Prelude: Stealing the Boat' and 'Storm on the Island' have much in common. Both use vivid imagery to show that nature can be a frightening force, and both demonstrate nature's power to alter the way people think, feel and behave. However, Wordsworth focuses on nature's power to shape the human personality, while in 'Storm on the Island' Heaney focuses on human resistance to nature's elemental forces.

Glossary

alliteration	Where words that are close together start with the same sound, e.g. "flowing flakes that flock".
ambiguity	Where a word or phrase has two or more possible interpretations.
assonance	When words share the same vowel sound but their consonants are different, e.g. "might fly our lives like paper kites".
autobiographical	Describing something that happened in the poet's life.
blank verse	Poetry written in iambic pentameter that doesn't rhyme.
caesura (plural caesurae)	A pause in a line of poetry. E.g. around the full stop in "Maps too. The sun shines through".
chronological	When events are arranged in the order in which they happened.
colloquial	Sounding like everyday spoken language, e.g. "One of my mates goes by".
consonance	Repetition of a consonant sound in nearby words, e.g. "numb as a smashed arm".
dialect	A variation of a language spoken by people from a particular place or background. Dialects might include different words or sentence constructions, e.g. "what happen to de Caribs".
dramatic monologue	A form of poetry that uses the assumed voice of a single speaker who is not the poet to address an implied audience, e.g. 'My Last Duchess'.
emotive	Something that makes you feel a particular emotion.
empathy	When someone understands what someone else is experiencing and how they feel about it.
end-stopping	Finishing a line of poetry with the end of a phrase or sentence.
enjambment	When a sentence or phrase runs over from one line or stanza to the next.
euphemism	An indirect word or phrase used instead of something upsetting or offensive, or to conceal meaning. E.g. the narrator of 'My Last Duchess' says "all smiles stopped" to avoid saying that his wife died.
first person	When a poet writes about themselves or their group, using words like "I", "my", "we" and "our".
form	The type of poem, e.g. a sonnet or a ballad, and its features, like number of lines, rhyme and rhythm.
free verse	Poetry that doesn't rhyme and has no regular rhythm or line length.
half-rhymes	Words that have a similar, but not identical, end sound. E.g. "crisp" and "grasp".
homonyms	Words that are spelt and pronounced the same, but have different meanings, e.g. "tissue".
iambic pentameter	Poetry with a metre of ten syllables — five of them stressed, and five unstressed. The stress falls on every second syllable, e.g. "That's my last Duchess painted on the wall".
iambic tetrameter	Like iambic pentameter but with a metre of eight syllables — four stressed and four unstressed. E.g. "But most through midnight streets I hear".
imagery	Language that creates a picture in your mind. It includes metaphors, similes and personification.
in medias res	When a narrative starts in the middle of the action, e.g. 'Bayonet Charge'.
internal rhyme	When two or more words in the same line rhyme, e.g. "tears between the bath and pre-lunch beers".
irony	When words are used to imply the opposite of what they normally mean. It can also mean when there is a difference between what people expect and what actually happens.
juxtaposition	When a poet puts two ideas, events, characters or descriptions close to each other to encourage the reader to contrast them. E.g. Agard juxtaposes figures from British and Caribbean history.
language	The choice of words used. Different kinds of language have different effects.
layout	The way a piece of poetry is visually presented to the reader, e.g. line length, how the poem is broken up into different stanzas, whether lines create some kind of visual pattern.

Glossary

metaphor	A way of describing something by saying that it is something else, e.g. "the loose silver of whitebait".
metre	The arrangement of stressed and unstressed syllables to create rhythm in a line of poetry.
monologue	One person speaking for a long period of time.
mood	The feel or atmosphere of a poem, e.g. humorous, threatening, eerie.
narrative	Writing that tells a story, e.g. 'The Charge of the Light Brigade'.
narrator	The person speaking the words. E.g. the narrator of 'Poppies' is a mother whose son has gone to war.
onomatopoeia	A word that sounds like the thing it's describing, e.g. "rumbles" and "jingle" in 'Exposure'.
oral poetry	Poetry that is intended to be spoken aloud, rather than read.
oxymoron	A phrase which appears to contradict itself, e.g. "marriage hearse".
personification	Describing a non-living thing as if it has human qualities and feelings, or behaves in a human way, e.g. "My city hides behind me."
Petrarchan sonnet	A form of sonnet in which the first eight lines have a regular ABBA rhyme scheme and introduce a problem, while the final six lines have a different rhyme scheme and solve the problem.
phonetic spellings	When words are spelt as they sound rather than with their usual spelling, e.g. "dem" instead of "them". It's often used to show that someone is speaking with a certain accent or dialect.
plosive	A short burst of sound made when you say a word containing the letters b, d, g, k, p or t.
rhetoric	Language used by the poet to persuade you of a particular view.
rhetorical question	A question that doesn't need an answer, but is asked to make or emphasise a point.
rhyme scheme	A pattern of rhyming words in a poem. E.g. 'London' has an ABAB rhyme scheme — this means that the first and third lines in each stanza rhyme, and so do the second and fourth lines.
rhyming couplet	A pair of rhyming lines that are next to each other, e.g. the last two lines of 'War Photographer'.
rhyming triplet	Three rhyming lines that are next to each other, e.g. lines 13-15 of 'The Charge of the Light Brigade'.
rhythm	A pattern of sounds created by the arrangement of stressed and unstressed syllables.
sibilance	Repetition of 's' and 'sh' sounds, e.g. "sentries whisper, curious, nervous".
simile	A way of describing something by comparing it to something else, usually by using the words "like" or "as", e.g. "the world overflowing / like a treasure chest".
sonnet	A form of poem with fourteen lines, that usually follows a clear rhyme scheme.
stanza	A group of lines in a poem.
structure	The order and arrangement of ideas and events in a poem, e.g. how it begins, develops and ends.
syllable	A single unit of sound within a word. E.g. "all" has one syllable, "always" has two.
symbolism	When an object stands for something else. E.g. the statue of Ozymandias symbolises human power, and the dove in 'Poppies' symbolises mourning.
syntax	The arrangement of words in a sentence or phrase so that they make sense.
third person	When a poet writes about a character who isn't the speaker, using words like "he" or "she".
tone	The mood or feelings suggested by the way the narrator writes, e.g. confident, thoughtful.
voice	The characteristics of the person narrating the poem. Poems are usually written either using the poet's voice, as if they're speaking to you directly, or the voice of a character.
volta	A turning point in a poem, when the argument or tone changes dramatically.

Index

A

absence 5, 13, 21, 29, 40
alliteration 2, 12, 20, 24, 52, 75
ambiguity 21, 22, 45, 57, 65
anger 5, 23, 31, 36, 42, 55, 70, 73
arrogance 2, 3, 7, 36, 43, 76
art 3, 9, 43, 57
assonance 12, 14-16, 52

B

'Bayonet Charge' 11, 13, 15-17, 19, 23, 33, 38, 39, 43, 45, 51, 52, 54, 56, 57, 63, 67-69
Biblical references 10, 12, 22
blank verse 7, 15

C

caesurae 6, 12, 14-18, 20, 21, 50, 54, 68, 76
'Charge of the Light Brigade, The' 10, 11, 13, 17, 32, 38-40, 44, 49, 50, 52, 54-56, 63
'Checking Out Me History' 9, 29-31, 34, 36, 42, 44, 49, 53-55, 65, 73
colloquial language 18, 19, 39, 55
confidence 7, 43, 56, 58, 76
consonance 24, 52
context 65
contrasts 5, 6, 16, 18, 23, 36, 50, 51, 75
control 8, 9, 25, 36, 55
Crimean War 11, 30

D

direct address 14, 15, 24, 57
direct speech 28, 29, 55
dramatic monologues 5, 9, 45, 49
Duke Alfonso II of Ferrara 8

E

effects of conflict 11, 17, 19, 21, 23, 38, 70, 71
'Emigrée, The' 5, 15, 21, 26, 27, 34, 38, 40, 41, 45, 50, 51, 53, 56, 58, 65, 74
emotive language 5, 22, 23, 42, 70, 71
end-stopping 14, 27, 50, 56
enjambment 8, 9, 14, 17, 18, 21, 23-25, 27, 28, 50, 54, 68, 75, 76
'Exposure' 3, 7, 11-13, 17, 33, 37-40, 43, 49, 52-54, 56-58, 65, 67-69

F

fear 6, 7, 15, 17, 21, 38, 42, 43, 52, 58, 68, 69, 75, 76
first-person narrators 4-7, 13, 15, 19, 21, 27, 42, 55, 68
forms of poetry 49
freedom 21, 24, 25, 40, 50, 52, 54
French Revolution 4, 69

G

guilt 6, 19, 42, 45, 71

H

half-rhymes 12, 13, 68
helplessness 15, 54
heritage 24, 30, 31, 44, 57
heroism 11, 39, 44, 51, 52, 54
homonyms 25
hopelessness 5, 13, 39, 43, 58, 68, 69
human achievement 2, 3, 51

I

iambic pentameter 3, 7
identity 21, 25, 28-31, 44
imagery 14-23, 28, 29, 39, 53, 58, 68-70, 75
individual experiences 5, 7, 19, 23, 27, 45
in medias res 17, 43, 56
irony 2, 3, 22, 28-30, 36, 51, 56, 69

K

'Kamikaze' 19, 21, 23, 27-29, 34, 37, 38, 40, 41, 44, 51, 55, 57, 74

L

Lady Macbeth 18, 42
light 24-27, 30, 31, 37, 51, 53, 75
'London' 4, 5, 13, 15, 27, 31, 32, 36, 40, 42, 43, 45, 51, 54, 57, 73
loss 5, 13, 21, 26, 27, 40, 51

M

memory 19, 23, 26-29, 41, 53, 55, 71, 74
metaphors 6, 12, 15, 18, 22, 26, 29, 30, 36, 38, 41, 43, 53, 64, 68-71, 73
monosyllabic words 15, 22, 41, 54, 57
mood 54, 58
'My Last Duchess' 3, 8, 9, 32, 36, 40, 43, 49, 54, 55, 57

N

'Napalm Girl' 22
nature 3, 6, 7, 12-15, 28-30, 37, 45, 56, 68, 69
nostalgia 27, 40

O

onomatopoeia 10, 12, 16, 39, 52, 63
oral poetry 31, 65
oxymorons 4, 6, 14
'Ozymandias' 2, 3, 9, 25, 32, 36, 37, 43, 49, 51, 54, 56

P

pain 23, 38, 39, 41, 42, 51
patriotism 11, 16, 28, 29, 39, 44, 69
P.E.E.D. 63, 70
personification 6, 10, 12, 13, 15, 26, 27, 37, 43, 45, 53, 58, 68, 69, 74, 75
phonetic spellings 30, 31, 55
plosive sounds 14, 22, 52, 53
'Poppies' 11, 19-21, 25, 27, 29, 33, 38, 40, 41, 44, 51-53, 55, 64
power of humans 2, 3, 5, 9, 25, 31, 36, 40, 42, 51
power of nature 3, 6, 7, 12, 13, 15, 25, 29, 36, 37, 58, 75, 76
'Prelude, The: Stealing the Boat' 3, 5-7, 15, 17, 29, 32, 37, 41, 43, 45, 52, 53, 57, 58, 75, 76
pride 3, 8, 9, 24, 29, 42, 43, 57
propaganda 28, 44

R

reality of conflict 11, 13, 17, 39, 68, 69
religious imagery 20, 22-24, 58, 70
'Remains' 7, 11, 18, 19, 23, 33, 38, 39, 41, 42, 45, 50, 53, 55-58, 70, 71
repetition 4, 5, 8, 10, 11, 18-20, 24, 26, 28, 30, 31, 37, 42, 44, 50, 52, 58, 71
rhetoric 5, 42
rhetorical questions 10, 12, 13, 39
rhyme 9, 11, 36, 49, 54, 57, 68, 71
Romanticism 2, 3, 6, 56, 65

S

senses 5, 20, 21, 26, 40, 41, 51
sibilance 6, 10, 12, 14, 15, 18, 22, 28, 52, 68, 69
similes 6, 14-16, 20, 22, 24, 28, 29, 53, 58, 75
'Songs of Innocence and Experience' 4
sound 4, 51, 52
Stormont 14
'Storm on the Island' 3, 7, 13-15, 33, 36, 37, 43, 52, 53, 56-58, 75, 76
spoken language 55
suffering 5, 13, 49, 54, 69, 70
symbolism 12, 20
syntax 30, 31, 55

T

third-person narrators 11, 29, 55, 57, 68
'Tissue' 24, 25, 31, 34, 36, 37, 44, 50, 52, 57

V

voice 55
voltas 3, 15, 18, 19, 22, 75, 76

W

'War Photographer' 11, 19, 21-23, 34, 38, 39, 41, 42, 45, 49, 55, 57, 58, 70, 71

Answers

These are the answers to the exercises in Section Five. They're only suggestions, so don't worry if what you've written doesn't match exactly — there are lots of possible answers.

Page 70 — Adding Quotes and Developing Points

Sample Plan

(A) "sneer of cold command"

(B) "Look on my works, ye Mighty, and despair!"

(C) "That's my last Duchess painted on the wall"

(D) "Then all smiles stopped together."

(E) The collapse of the ruler's "works" suggests that power is fleeting, which makes the reader question their own attitude towards power.

(F) The Duke's coldness and complete control is unsettling, and the reader is left in little doubt that the Duke had his wife killed.

Answer Extract 1

(A) "he's there on the ground, sort of inside out"

(B) "the image of agony"

(C) "running children in a nightmare heat"

Answer Extract 2

(A) "probably armed, possibly not"

(B) "a priest preparing to intone a Mass"

(C) "All flesh is grass."

Page 71 — Adding Quotes and Developing Points

Answer Extract 1

(A) Using the term "enemy" gives an indication of the potential threat that the memory holds for the soldier.

(B) The photographer and the bereaved wife are affected by the conflict in very different ways, but this painful image helps the reader to empathise with both of them.

Answer Extract 2

(A) This irregular form creates a disjointed experience for the reader, giving them a sense of the soldier's disrupted state of mind.

(B) Through this regular form, Duffy creates something ordered from the chaos of war, just as the photographer does through his photographs.

Answer Extract 3

(A) In the first stanza this phrase isn't dwelt on and is part of the easygoing, colloquial tone. However, when it's repeated it is a sinister reminder of the soldier's questionable actions.

(B) Duffy subverts the traditional notion of home as a refuge — home offers no comfort and instead forces him to confront his memories and guilt.

Page 73 — Marking Answer Extracts

Answer Extract 1

I think this answer would get a grade 4-5 because it makes a point comparing the two poems and supports the point with quotes from the poems. To get a higher grade it needs to develop the ideas more fully and explain the effect of the quotes in more detail.

Answer Extract 2

I would give this answer a grade 8-9 because it gives a detailed analysis of the poets' use of language, uses the correct technical vocabulary and offers different interpretations of the phrase "black'ning church".

Answer Extract 3

I think this answer would get a grade 6-7. It makes a good point comparing the poems, and it suggests what the impact on the reader might be. To get a higher grade, the effect of the quotes needs to be explained in more detail.

Page 74 — Marking Answer Extracts

Answer Extract 1

I would give this extract a grade 6-7 because it makes a point, gives examples from the text and starts to analyse language. To get a higher grade, the point needs to be developed more, e.g. it could comment on the effect on the reader.

Answer Extract 2

I think this answer would get a grade 4-5. This is because it makes points about the poems and backs them up with examples that are briefly explained. To get a higher grade it needs to offer more explanation of how the quotes support the point.

Answer Extract 3

I think this answer would get a grade 8-9 because it integrates examples from the poems and explains them effectively. It also includes some relevant knowledge of context.

Pages 75-76 — Marking a Whole Answer

I think this answer should be awarded a grade 8-9 because it makes a wide range of detailed comparisons and focuses on the effects of form, structure and language on the reader. It also makes relevant references to context, uses a range of technical vocabulary, and gives well-explained examples of the poets' techniques.

ACHR43